The Complete Guide

To

Airgunning

By

Jeffrey Guinan

The Complete Guide to Airgunning

ISBN 978-0-9822830-0-4

Printed in the United States of America

CONTENTS

INTRODUCTION

WARNING: There are those who can indulge in casual airgunning, as some indulge in casual drug use, but many hapless souls become addicted to this hobby once they get that first adult airgun.

True, a Daisy BB gun may not lead a 9-year-old down the path of perdition, but a quiet, accurate, powerful English or German airgun, an amalgam of richly-blued steel and polished wood, can ignite a craving for more and more of these wonderful weapons. Soon, like any addict, the afflicted airgunner is hiding new purchases from an irate spouse, or juggling funds to finance the next totally unnecessary addition to an ever-growing collection.

This guide to airgunning may, in fact, be socially irresponsible. It may promote the addiction by exposing the unsuspecting airgunner to new aspects of this fascinating hobby, or, worse, it may lure a hapless newcomer – someone merely looking for advice on a cheap rat or pigeon eliminator – into a lifelong search for Tyrolean-stocked Walthers or Sheridan Supergrades. Thankfully, this guide doesn't cover all airguns in production today (the sensory overload would be devastating, and new guns seem to emerge weekly), but that's not its purpose anyway.

The purpose of this guide is to give the reader an understanding of the fundamentals of airgunning, an understanding that will likely be as applicable ten years from now as it is today. Yes, some new form of propulsion system may come along tomorrow, but it will likely be a variation on an existing system. The vaunted pre-charged pneumatics that burst onto the scene a few years back – those expensive powerhouses that can exceed rimfires in power and accuracy – are old hat. Austrian soldiers in the late 1700s used air rifles fitted with removable flasks that provided enough man-killing power for 20 quick shots at ranges to 100 yards. The flasks for these 50-caliber repeaters were recharged by heavy-duty pumps carried on horse-drawn caissons. So much for the *new* pre-charged airguns. The latest variation on this theme is a rifle that can be powered by both pre-charged air or bulk CO_2.

So be assured that this guide will not quickly be outdated simply because new airguns hit the market each week. There are only a few basic propulsion systems and a few basic sighting systems, all of which require little more than a pleasant evening's reading for familiarization. It is the various permutations, combinations, styles, and accessories that account for the myriad of airguns available today. Familiarizing oneself with those is not the work of an evening, but of a lifetime. It's not really *work*, of course. Airguns are not only fascinating in and of themselves – and there are many proud owners who rarely shoot their treasures – but instruments capable of such precision that they'll continually and happily challenge a marksman's ability, no matter how good he or she may become.

AIRGUN PROJECTILES

The word *projectile* encompasses all the various types of objects shot by airguns, of which the vaunted diabolo pellet forms but one group. The first airgun projectiles were probably the clay balls and reed darts used in the blowguns depicted on the walls of ancient Egyptian tombs, and their use likely predates recorded history. As time passed, humans developed a greater variety of projectile launchers. Some of these devices used gunpowder, others used compressed air, and one, the Perkins machine gun of 1824, was powered by steam. The projectiles used in these weapons were usually identical in all respects but size, and they were typically made of lead because its density and malleability most efficiently carried the weapon's energy to the target.

Although lead has fallen into disfavor as a projectile material in some quarters, and is even legally banned for use in American waterfowling, it is still the predominant metal used in manufacturing airgun pellets. Some companies, perhaps seeing the handwriting on the wall, have begun to produce pellets made of non-poisonous alloys. These harder metals would ordinarily damage the rifling in airgun barrels, so the pellets are encased in plastic sleeves. These lightweight contrivances travel at higher velocities than their heavier lead counterparts and, being resistant to deformation, manage to penetrate animate and inanimate targets to impressive depths. However, efficient killing is not simply a matter of penetration, as will be discussed more fully in the chapters on hunting with the airgun.

Ballistic Coefficient

A small, steel BB will zip out of the muzzle of an airgun at a much higher velocity than a heavier lead BB of the same size, but the lead BB will travel farther and deliver more of its original energy to the target. This capacity to retain energy over distance is one of the characteristics captured in a projectile's numerical ballistic coefficient (BC), which is, among other things, a measurement of an object's drag as it flies through the air. The higher the BC, the farther the projectile may be expected to fly, and the less it will be affected by crosswinds, all other factors being equal. In general, the more streamlined the projectile, the higher its BC (indicated for various pellets in Table 1).

Currently, the two most popular airgun calibers are .177 and .22. Although each has its rabid devotees, it can't be denied that a .22 pellet traveling at 500 fps will have more energy than a .177 pellet traveling at 500 fps, if the .22 is the heavier pellet. This ballistic fact should be considered by airgunners in countries that limit air weapons by velocity rather than energy.

Darts and Bolts

Outside of their use in blowguns, darts are something of an oddity in airgunning today. Although they were once used in extremely accurate parlor airguns made for the wealthy in late 19th century America, they are today noted  primarily for their use in low-powered training pistols that are sold with an accompanying dartboard.

Bolts are a relatively recent entrant into the world of airgun projectiles. They can be used in any open-breeched rifle or pistol without fear of damage to rifling, due to the plastic band that is of greater diameter than the hard metal core.

Diabolo Pellets

It is the diabolo pellet that is most frequently associated with serious airgunning. The name derives from the shape of a once-popular toy that operated much like a yo-yo. In later times, the term wasp-waisted was applied to these pellets. Although the  design of the pellet's head, or forward end, varies considerably, the center area is narrowly constricted and the rear portion is hollow, forming what is called the pellet's *skirt*. The first projectile to use a hollow base was the conical lead bullet designed in the 1840s by Frenchman Claude Minié (min-yay), who wanted a projectile that would not only drop quickly

Table 1. Pellet Weights, Ballistic Coefficients

PELLET	Cal	Wt.	Type	BC	PELLET	Cal	Wt.	Type	BC
Beeman Silver Bear	.177	7.10	HP	.019	Beeman Laser	.177	6.5	R	.008
	.20	9.60	HP	.017		.20	9.4	R	.012
	.22	12.6	HP	.012		.22	13.0	R	.010
	.25	26.7	HP	.018		.25	17.6	R	.008
Beeman Silver Jet	.177	8.1	P	.020	Marksman FTS	.177	8.8	R	.017
	.20	10.7	P	.020		.20	11.1	R	.026
	.22	15.2	P	.017		.22	15.0	R	.022
Beeman Silver Sting	.177	8.4	P	.015	RWS Hobby	.177	6.9	F	.009
	.20	10.5	P	.016		.22	12.0	F	.010
	.22	15.8	P	.015	RWS Supermag	.177	9.5	F	.012
	.25	25.1	P	.019	RWS Meisterkugeln	.177	8.3	F	.011
Beeman Crow Magnum	.177	8.8	HP	.012		.22	13.9	F	.012
	.20	12.6	HP	.015	RWS Superpoint	.177	8.3	P	.011
	.22	18.6	HP	.014		.22	14.5	P	.013
	.25	26.0	HP	.016	RWS Super-H-Point	.177	7.4	HP	.010
Beeman Silver Arrow	.177	11.9	P	.016		.22	13.9	HP	.011
	.20	16.0	P	.012	RWS Superdome	.177	8.3	R	.014
	.22	17.0	P	.017		.22	14.5	R	.013
	.25	24.6	P	.019	H&N Match	.177	8.2	F	.016
Beeman Kodiak	.177	10.6	R	.021		.22	13.8	F	.011
	.20	13.3	R	.029	Sheridan Cylindrical	.20	15.1	R	.023
	.22	21.1	R	.031	Beeman Perfect Round	.177	8.02	LS	.014
	.25	30.7	R	.035		.25	23.6	LS	.020
Crosman Premier	.177	7.9	R	.024	Bisley Superfield	.177	8.5	RH	.019
	.177	10.5	R	.032		.20	11.5	RH	.020
	.20	14.3	R	.047		.22	15.0	RH	.016
	.22	14.3	R	0.33		.25	24.6	RH	.024

down the fouled barrel of a muzzleloading military rifle during the frenzy of battle, but fire accurately once loaded. The principle that made this projectile so successful in the US Civil War applies equally to its success in airgunning. The thin-walled, hollow base bulges outward when filled with expanding air or CO_2. This expansion serves two purposes: it seals the propellant behind the projectile, preventing power-robbing gas leakage; and it drives the lead walls into the rifling, imparting the stabilizing axial spin so necessary for accuracy.

The design of the diabolo pellet's head has evolved over time, settling into a few distinct categories. Although it can be said that each design it best suited for a particular type of airgun shooting (flatheads for match shooting, for example), experienced airgunners will generally use whatever type shoots most accurately in his or her gun, especially if used for hunting. Discovering a particular gun's preferred diet is a matter of experimentation, an activity made more convenient by purchasing so-called *sampler packs*. These samplers provide a small quantity of each pellet type, segregated by compartments in a single package. It's an inexpensive way to try a variety of pellets. The various styles of airgun pellets are described in the sections that follow.

Roundhead

Roundheads, or domes, are probably the most useful, all-around pellet style and likely

account for the greatest number of pellets sold. Most shooters find that a roundhead pellet will deliver the greatest accuracy at extended

*Roundheads
.177; .20; 22 (l-r)*

ranges, as well as the deepest penetration.

Flathead

Flathead pellets cut a sharp, distinct hole in a paper target. Such holes are easier to score than the jagged tears made by other

pellet styles. The remaining cut-outs (i.e., chads) resemble wads, giving rise to another moniker for this style, *wadcutter*. Shooters often discover that flatheads are the most accurate pellet

*Flatheads
.177; .22*

for a particular gun, but hunters find an advantage, too, in that flatheads, with their limited penetration, can transmit more of a pellet's energy to a living target than designs that "icepick" their way clean through the animal. Flatheads tend to be lighter than other pellets and will usually give the highest initial velocity from a particular gun, though they shed that speed quickly once launched. These high velocity readings make flatheads the preferred "marketing pellet" for manufacturers seeking to advertise high velocities for their wares (without mentioning, of course, the weight of the pellet in their ads). Another advantage of the flathead style is its ability to feed smoothly in repeaters that stack the pellets in their magazines.

Pointed Pellets

Pointed pellets are often the first choice for hunters, and they can indeed penetrate more deeply than other styles, all things being equal. Sometimes it is only the pointed pellet that can get through the tough feather "shield" of a pigeon or crow sitting

Pointeds .177 and .22

broadside to the hunter. Some shooters have found, though, that the superior penetration is offset by the fact that the pointed pellet may not be as accurate as other styles at extended ranges. This is not a hard-and-fast rule, however, and a conscientious hunter will conduct both accuracy and penetration experiments, at various ranges and with assorted pellet styles, before venturing afield.

Hollow Points

Over the years, the term *hollow point* has garnered a sinister cachet - not unlike *dum-dum* and *full-metal jacket* – and that may be the reason they were first

Hollowpoints .177; .22

introduced to airgunners, many of whom were boys wishing they had a firearm rather than a pellet gun. The fact is, a hollow-pointed projectile is designed to expand (mushroom) as it travels through a living target, thereby increasing shock and tissue damage, and this expansion requires a velocity not often reached by the average airgun. They can indeed be effective on game when launched from high-powered

sporters, but are of little practical use in most airguns.

Perhaps because of this, manufacturers have created a hybrid hollow-pointed pellet that incorporates a sharp plastic point nestled in its nose. In practice, this plastic point not only enhances penetration, but, driven rearward as it traverses the animal's flesh, it assists in expanding the head of the pellet and creating a significantly larger wound channel than would a non-expanding pellet.

Cylindricals

Although they are not diabolos because of their straight walls, cylindrical pellets do have a hollow base. Probably the most recognizable cylindrical in airgunning is the .20-caliber pellet used in the original

Cylindricals 16-gr (l); 14-gr both .20

Sheridan pump pneumatic rifles. Cylindricals offer greater weight than diabolo pellets of comparable length. This translates into greater energy retention, which is likely why it was chosen by the developers of the Sheridan. The original 16-grain Sheridan pellet was made of a harder alloy than pure lead pellets and offered greater penetration. The current offering is slightly waisted, lighter by nearly 2 grains, and is made of softer alloy.

Balls

Balls were the first airgun projectiles. The .175 copper-flashed BB beloved by young boys is produced in the billions yearly, while heavy .30 and .40 caliber

Balls: .175 steel (BB); .177 lead; .25 lead (l-r)

lead balls are launched with deer-killing power from large pre-charged pneumatics. Pump CO_2 airguns of recent vintage used .22 and .25 caliber lead balls not only because they delivered a more telling blow than lighter pellets, but because they fed properly in repeating mechanisms.

The steel BB is an inefficient missile for anything but close-range plinking and target work. Some shooters can increase the effectiveness of their BB guns by switching to lead BBs, but such balls don't necessarily feed well, if at all, in repeaters designed for steel ammo.

Some early pneumatics, notably the Apache rifle and pistol, used .25-caliber lead balls to great effect on game. Owners of these weapons today use #4 buckshot to keep their weapons from being wall-hangers.

Plastic-sheathed, lead-free pellets; assembled .177 and .22 pellets shown at left.

Hybrid Pellets

Hybrid pellets combine various materials to achieve greater velocity and penetration than pellets made solely of lead or lead alloy. The first of these hybrids were plastic-sheathed pellets that used a hard metal core (for deep penetration) encased in a lightweight sheath (to "take" the rifling and boost velocity). The same principle applies to lead pellets that use either a hard metal ball or a sharply pointed polymer "spear" in their noses.

Shotshells for a spring-powered shotgun; components at right. Daisy BB shown for scale.

Shotshells

Air shotguns have been developed and sold commercially, but have never been successful, primarily because of poor performance. Defunct manufacturers include Vincent, Paul, Giffard, and Yewha. Some of these pneumatic guns used reloadable shells, others used chalk cylinders that disintegrated upon firing and released their embedded shot. Crosman produced a CO_2-powered shotgun, but discontinued it soon after introduction. A spring-powered shotgun currently produced in Europe uses the non-reloadable shells shown above.

.22 polymer-tipped pellet at left; .177 lead pellet at right has copper ball in nose. Both systems increase penetration and expansion in game.

PROPULSION SYSTEMS

The Spring Gun

Description

A spring gun uses a spring-driven piston in a cylinder to compress air that drives a projectile from the weapon (figure below shows components). The projectile may be a ball, a waisted or conical pellet, a bolt, or a dart. Spring rifles and pistols are currently produced in the following calibers: .175 (BB), .177, .20, .22, .25, and .30. Spring guns span all levels of sophistication, power, and cost, ranging from the folded-metal BB guns of the Red Ryder type to the magnificent match guns that collected Olympic gold before the advent of pre-charged pneumatics (PCPs). This category also includes very large and potent small game sporter rifles that can generate upwards of 25 foot pounds of energy (fpe).

Spring rifles and pistols are produced as single-shot and repeating weapons. Single-shot guns must be loaded and cocked by the shooter for each shot. A repeater incorporates a magazine that stores projectiles and loads them into the breech, but the shooter must cock the gun for each shot. Most Daisy BB guns are repeaters, with some of them storing as many as 1000 BBs in their magazines.

Operation

Cocking. As stated, the mainspring must be cocked for each shot. Cocking requires pushing or pulling the spring in its compression cylinder (see figure below) until the piston can be caught and restrained by the trigger sear. Cocking requires a lever of some sort and as much as 60 pounds of force, depending on the strength of the spring and the length of the cocking lever. Be advised that the cocking lever can snap back and harm the shooter if accidentally released before completion of the cocking and loading cycles. For this reason, knowledgeable shooters maintain a tight grip on the lever, not only until the sear engages the piston head and restrains the spring, but even during pellet loading. Some guns are fitted with ratcheting "anti-bear-trap" mechanisms that are intended to prevent smashed fingers or bent barrels should the cocking lever slip from the shooter's grasp, but these devices, like all gun safety mechanisms, can fail and should not be trusted.

Loading. Most barrelcockers are loaded by seating the pellet directly into the breech. Some require that the pellet be first dropped into a tap, which is then rotated to align the pellet with the bore. Upon firing, the pellet jumps from the tap into the bore. Some guns have spring-loaded pellet magazines that automatically introduce a pellet into the breech when the gun is cocked. The common BB gun typically has a reservoir for several hundred rounds and often relies on a magnet for holding each ball in the breech before firing.

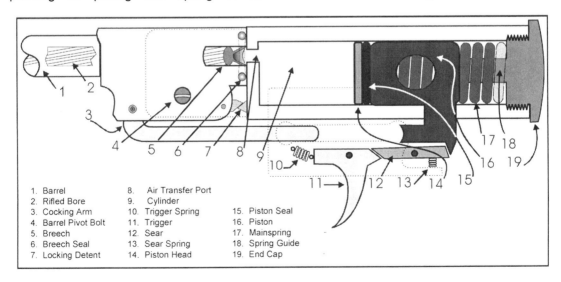

1. Barrel	8. Air Transfer Port	
2. Rifled Bore	9. Cylinder	
3. Cocking Arm	10. Trigger Spring	15. Piston Seal
4. Barrel Pivot Bolt	11. Trigger	16. Piston
5. Breech	12. Sear	17. Mainspring
6. Breech Seal	13. Sear Spring	18. Spring Guide
7. Locking Detent	14. Piston Head	19. End Cap

Typical spring gun components. Gun shown cocked.

Barrelcocking or "breakbarrel" spring rifle: Birmingham Small Arms (BSA) Supersport; .22 cal single shot; ~695 fps with 14.3 gr. pellet; 41 inches; 6 lbs.; beech stock; open rear, hooded front sight (shown with aftermarket rear aperture sight and globe front sight with interchangeable inserts); grooved scope ramp for 14 mm scope mounts (requires mounts larger than typical 12 mm mounts). Inset shows gun cocked and ready for loading.

Firing. To initiate the firing sequence, the shooter squeezes the trigger, which nudges the sear out of engagement with the piston, releasing it. The piston surges forward, compressing the air in the cylinder and forcing it through a transfer port into the barrel breech, where a projectile awaits. If the projectile is a pellet, its hollow base fills with air and spreads the skirt outward into the rifling, which is a set of spiraling lands and grooves cut or pressed into the inner surface of the barrel. The rifling causes the pellet to spin on its axis, a stabilizing influence that enhances accuracy[1]. The pellet races down the barrel atop an expanding column of air until it leaps free of the gun.

Variations

Each of the variations described below is illustrated in this section.

Barrelcockers. Barrelcocking spring guns use the barrel as the lever that pushes or pulls the spring into compression. In this design, the barrel is usually positioned in line with the compression cylinder, allowing the air to take a relatively straight, and thus more efficient, path to the base of the projectile. In this design, the piston moves away from the shooter during firing.

Overlevers. In this variation, the barrel is positioned over the compression cylinder, making for a relatively compact weapon. Overlevers are a subclass of the barrelcocking family, in that the barrel is used to draw the mainspring into

compression. In this design, the projectile is loaded directly into the breech and the piston moves toward the shooter during firing.

Sidelevers. Sidelever spring guns use a separate lever, positioned alongside the compression chamber, to cock the mainspring. In this design the barrel is in front of the compression chamber, but is locked in place; in traditional barrelcockers, the barrel swings during cocking. The sidelever's barrel/receiver rigidity is considered by some to make for a more accurate weapon than a barrelcocker, where barrel lockup is accomplished by either spring-loaded detents or locking mechanisms that must be released by the shooter. In a sidelever, the projectile is loaded directly into the breech, or into a magazine that positions the projectile in line with the breech. The piston moves away from the shooter during firing.

Underlevers. Unlike barrelcockers, underlever airguns have a barrel permanently affixed to the compression chamber. The spring is cocked by a lever positioned under the barrel. Some of the earliest, commercially successful spring guns were underlevers produced in England.

Concentric Spring Guns. In this design, the barrel runs through the center of the piston and spring. At firing, the piston is released and rushes rearward, compressing the air ahead of it. The air reaches the rear of the gun where it hits the end cap, reverses direction, and enters the breech. There, the blast encounters a pellet waiting in the chamber. The air launches the pellet down the barrel and out of the gun. As with

---

[1] Some airgun barrels have a "choke," a deliberately-narrowed section at the muzzle that constricts the pellet just before it leaves the gun. This is believed to increase accuracy.

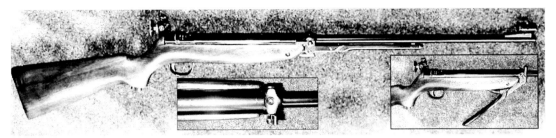

Underlever spring rifle: Webley & Scott Mark III Supertarget: .177 cal single shot; 43 inches; ~7 lbs; walnut stock; aperture sight; ~ 600 fps with 8-gr pellet. Left inset shows tap-loading hole; lever up, ready for pellet insertion. Right inset shows underlever at end of cocking stroke.

the overlever, the concentric configuration permits the use of a relatively longer spring and cylinder (as compared to a gun with the barrel ahead of the compression cylinder), which can mean greater power in a smaller package. Concentric airguns appear to have been produced only as pistols, perhaps because the awkward cocking stroke does not translate well to a rifle-sized weapon. The gun is cocked by pressing a button to release the top half of the gun, then pulling upward on the barrel/spring unit until the sear clicks into engagement, restraining the spring. The top is then lowered back to the grip and snapped into place. The pellet is loaded from the rear of the gun where, typically, a panel or shutter moves aside, allowing a pellet to be dropped directly into the breech.

Gas "Spring" Guns. A variation of the spring gun design utilizes a so-called gas spring (shown below). The "spring" is actually a pocket of trapped gas, usually air, that is encased within an outer sleeve. This outer sleeve slides back and forth within a compression cylinder in a manner similar to the piston in a typical coil spring gun. The outer sleeve also serves as the piston and is fitted with a seal. During the cocking stroke, this piston is pushed back to compress the gas within. At the end of the cocking stroke, a sear catches and restrains

the piston. When the trigger is pulled, the piston surges forward in the compression cylinder, compressing the air ahead of it and driving the pellet out of the barrel.

The gas spring has several advantages over a traditional metal spring: the gas won't take a "set" if the gun remains cocked for an extended period, making it attractive to hunters who leave their guns cocked for long periods; the gas will not lose its resiliency over time; there is no vibration or noise from the expanding gas; and it is believed to have a faster "lock time" than a comparable coil-spring gun. "Lock time," when applied to an airgun, refers to the time a pellet spends in the gun once the trigger has released the sear. Because a spring gun moves before the pellet has left the barrel, a shorter lock time means that the moving gun has less time to influence the path of the pellet. This is discussed further in the section *Managing Recoil in a Spring Gun.*

Some gas spring guns are supplied with a pump that allows the owner to increase the power of the gun by raising the pre-cocking pressure of the gas. Obviously, this also increases cocking effort and recoil. The pressure may be lowered by tapping a valve to release some of the gas; this reduces velocity but can make the gun easier to

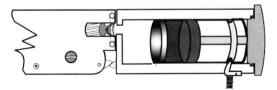

Cocked Gas Spring: Gas is compressed in its sealed cylinder; trigger sear is restraining piston; pellet loaded in breech.

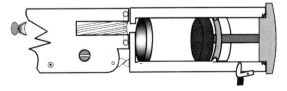

Fired Gas Spring: Trigger sear releases piston; expanding gas forces piston forward, compressing air that drives pellet from gun.

Gas spring (or gas "ram") The gas permanently sealed within the cylinder can be compressed (similar in concept to the cocking of a metallic spring). When the gas is allowed to decompress (similar to the releasing of a metallic spring), the air ahead of the moving cylinder then drives the pellet out of the gun.

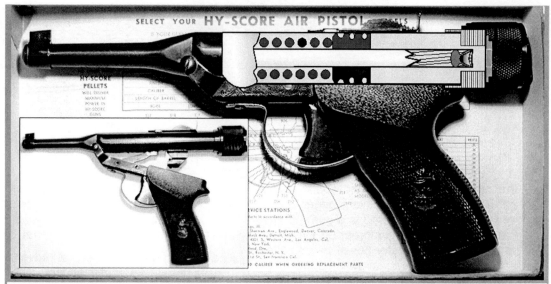

Concentric spring pistol: Hy-Score 802 shown lying in original box lid; 177 cal; 6-shot repeater; 10 ¾ inches overall; barrel length 10 inches; 2 lbs; rear sight adjustable for elevation; 450 fps with 7.9-gr pellet. Overlay depicts barrel going through center of spring and piston, a design permitting a compact pistol with a long cylinder and barrel. Piston travels rearward (to the right, in drawing) during firing. Inset shows how upper and lower segments separate for cocking. Knurled component at rear holds 6 pellets in individual chambers and is twisted to chamber a pellet prior to shooting.

cock and more pleasant to shoot. Many of the more popular coil-spring rifles can be retrofitted with a gas spring by a competent airgunsmith.

Managing Recoil in a Spring Gun

As stated, a spring gun moves, or *recoils*, during firing. This is the result of internal components in motion, particularly the piston. When released by the trigger and sear, the piston heads down the compression cylinder, cramming a large volume of air ahead of it into an ever smaller space. Near the end of its journey, the piston encounters a "block" of compressed air crowding around the narrow transfer port at the end of the cylinder. The piston actually bounces off this air, reversing direction. This rebound prevents the piston from damaging itself against the cylinder wall (which happens when unknowing shooters "dry" fire spring guns without a pellet in the breech), but the resulting backward/forward snap can be very pronounced (and annoying), especially if the gun is a light sporter with a powerful mainspring. Additionally, this peculiar recoil can damage the internal components of scope sights that are not airgun-rated (i.e., designed specifically to withstand the

backward/forward snap of spring-powered airguns). The recoil also loosens stock screws and can cause *scope creep* unless a scope stop (a block, screw, or peg-and-notch) prevents the scope from moving along the mounting rail. Additionally, heat is generated by the sudden compression of air in the cylinder. If a low-flash-point oil (i.e., oil that ignites at relatively low temperature) is present in the cylinder, transfer port, or barrel, it can ignite. The resulting explosion is called *dieseling*. Dieseling can produce noise, smoke, flame at the muzzle, higher-than-normal velocities, decreased accuracy, and piston damage.

Unless the gun has a recoil-cancelling feature, the barrel of a spring gun will momentarily move off point-of-aim before the pellet leaves the barrel, which means that the beer can, bullseye, or rat will not be hit unless the gun somehow returns to point-of-aim before the pellet leaves the gun. This improbable event can occur, providing the shooter resists the temptation to defeat recoil with a death grip and uses, instead, the so-called "Bronco Hold." A bronc-rider does not attempt to prevent his horse from bucking, nor does he try to cling to the animal by strength of arm or leg. Rather, he lets the animal gyrate as it wills

Recoilless spring rifle: Feinwerkbau 300; 177 cal.; single shot; 41 inches; 10 lbs; sidelever cocking; walnut stock; adjustable buttplate; micrometer aperture rear sight with rubber eyeshade; globe front sight with interchangeable inserts; grooved for scope; adjustable trigger; 640 fps with 7.9-gr pellets.

and conforms his own movements to those of the beast. In like manner, the spring gun shooter will hold the gun lightly at all points of contact and allow the gun to jump freely throughout the entire firing sequence. He will also hold his position steadily for a second or two after the pellet has left the barrel, which is called "maintaining the sight picture." In the Bronco Hold, the gun is held lightly at the forearm, which could mean letting it rest on an open palm; at the "wrist" of the stock, where the hand gently encircles the wood; at the shoulder, where the stock lightly touches the armpit; and at the trigger, where the pad of the fingertip gently presses on the curved blade. For consistency (the foundation of accuracy), the shooter will contact the gun in exactly the same place for each shot: the cheek should touch (lightly, remember) the same place on the stock, the palm must lie under the same patch of wood on the forearm, and so forth. Finding the right places is a matter of experimentation. The shooter may find, for example, that best accuracy is achieved by supporting the gun directly under the forearm screws, or perhaps an

inch before or after them, or that the thumb of the trigger hand should rest atop the wrist of the stock rather than alongside it. Experimentation is required.

The Bronco Hold applies to spring pistols as well as rifles. Whether the pistol is held in one hand or two, the principles are the same: hold the gun lightly, let it buck during firing, maintain sight picture until a second or two after the shot, hold the gun in the same place from shot-to-shot.

Spring Gun Tuning

"Tuning" is the process of modifying a spring gun to improve its manners. Magnum springers generate perhaps half the power of a high-velocity .22 short firearm cartridge but can be vastly more unpleasant to shoot due to harsh recoil and offensive metallic twanging. These deficiencies can be eliminated by the services of a good airgun tuner (search the net, keywords *airgun tuner*). Many low-powered springers can suffer the same problems and can benefit from a good tune. A tune can be as simple as applying heavy grease to the mainspring

Sidelever Spring Rifle: Russian IZH Model 61; .177; 5-shot removable clip magazine; slide-adjustable stock; 6 ¼ lb; 30-32in; open rear, globe front sights; grooved for scope; 450 fps with 7.9-gr pellet; anti-bear trap cocking. Inset: sidelever open at start of cocking stroke.

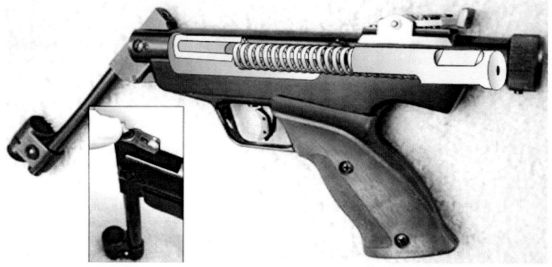

Recoilless breakbarrel spring pistol: RWS Model 6 using contra-motion pistons for recoil elimination. 177 cal; 16 inches; 3 lbs; adjustable trigger; adjustable rear sight with four rotating notches; globe front sight with interchangeable inserts; ~450 fps with 6-gr pellets. Overlay shows single mainspring with two pistons at either end that travel in opposing directions at instant of firing, cancelling recoil. Air compressed by front piston propels the pellet. Inset shows pellet insertion after cocking of spring.

via the cocking slot (a so-called "lube tune"), or as complicated as stripping the gun, replacing or modifying existing parts, creating new parts custom-matched to a particular gun, honing the chamber walls, installing front and rear spring guides, lubricating all components with specialized oils and greases, and re-assembling the gun. The effects of a complete, professional tune can be dramatic. Although tuning may reduce velocity slightly, the increase in shot-to-shot consistency and shooting pleasure invariably justifies the tradeoff. Some owners of magnum springers are astonished at how mannered their beast has become after a good tune, and it's generally accepted that a smooth-shooting springer is easier to shoot more accurately. Amateur tuners have done remarkable work with cheap chinese communist knock-offs, creating weapons that perform on par with the expensive European air weapons they've copied. The cost of a professional tune depends on the complexity of the work and the amount of custom or replacement parts created for a particular gun.

Recoilless Spring Guns

Despite their name, recoilless spring guns do recoil, but they either negate the effect of recoil, or isolate it from the shooter. They were developed originally to win gold

medals, and that they did, completely outclassing the recoiling target spring guns that preceded them. It is believed that most recoilless spring guns are sold to shooters who rarely, if ever, enter a match, but who appreciate the exceptional shooting aesthetics offered by these guns. Although they have been replaced on Olympic airgun firing lines by springless precharged pneumatics, they continue to be produced and sold in limited numbers. Their deeply blued metals and elegant walnut stocks are a fit accompaniment to their mechanical sophistication. Shooters report that cocking and firing these guns and feeling the smooth interplay of precisely machined components is pleasurable and relaxing in itself, no matter where the pellet holes ultimately appear on the target. These guns are typically of modest power and generate little noise, making them ideal for apartment dwellers. They are appreciated by a broad spectrum of shooters that includes basement paper-punchers, short-range vermin hunters, and even a few match shooters.

A recoilless spring gun compresses air in a manner similar to the recoilling spring gun, so the movement of piston and mainspring within a compression cylinder is essentially the same. They differ, however, in how they

Overlever spring pistol: Webley & Scott Tempest; 177 cal; single shot; 9 ins.; 2 lbs; black plastic grips (shown with mother-of-pearl grips once offered by Webley importer); adj. rear sight; adj. trigger; 425 fps with 7.9-gr pellet. Inset shows gun at end of cocking stroke, ready for pellet insertion into breech.

handle recoil. Early target spring guns relied on low-powered springs and heavy stocks (often lead-filled) to absorb recoil, but this was far from ideal and airgun engineers eventually developed various mechanisms to counteract recoil.

One of the first recoilless spring guns was the so-called contra-motion piston gun produced by Diana. This airgun used a secondary internal weight of equal mass (i.e., a second piston) that moved in the opposite direction of its counterpart at the other end of the mainspring. During firing, the two pistons leaped away from each other, one of them driving the pellet, the other cancelling the inertia of the first, leaving the gun virtually motionless.

Another design, by Anschutz, rather more complex, relied upon an oil-filled shock absorber to soak up recoil. Probably the most effective of all target spring guns, judging by medals won, are the superb sidecocking rifles and pistols from the Feinwerkbau corporation. Their guns use a simple but ingenious sledge system. The barrel and receiver form a single unit mounted on rails embedded in the stock. When the gun fires, the barrel and receiver unlock and recoil, but the slight movement occurs atop the rails and the shooter notices nothing. The parts of the gun held by the shooter remain motionless. The barrel/receiver unit must then be tilted forward and locked prior to cocking the gun for the next shot.

Care and Maintenance

Unless mistreated, a simple, robust spring gun can last for generations. Its springs and seals are subject to wear, of course, but these can last hundreds of thousands of shots and are readily replaced when necessary. There are many surviving examples of spring guns made in the early 1900s that are still looking and shooting as well as they did when new. In fact, some of them shoot better now because of advancements in spring design and metallurgy, and better seals, lubricants, and pellets.

Correct airgun handling (i.e., preventive maintenance) and lubrication are the essentials of airgun maintenance. Guidance in

Lubricating a spring gun chamber. Flexible oiling needle screws onto nozzle of oil bottle and allows inserting the needle into transfer port and placing drops precisely where needed within the compression chamber.

these areas is provided in manufacturer's manuals, but many airguns change hands without manuals. The information herein is a general guide to preventive maintenance and lubrication of the major components of the spring gun - compression chamber, spring, cocking linkages, barrel, and trigger - and should keep the average spring gun in optimal shooting condition. For additional information, contact manufacturers, distributors, airgunsmiths, and knowledgeable airgunners on online airgun forums.

Preventive Maintenance

A number of precautions can be taken to avoid problems:

Never fire a spring gun without a pellet. The piston needs the resistance of a chambered pellet to create the air cushion that prevents piston slap. Without this cushion, the spring-driven piston rams the far end of the chamber, with possible damage to the piston head. Obviously, one should never purchase an airgun from shops or individuals who "demonstrate" spring guns by "dry-firing" them.

Never use sub-caliber or deformed pellets. In other words, don't shoot .177 pellets in a .22 bore, or re-use fired pellets. Both could cause harmful piston slap.

Minimize the use of very lightweight pellets in magnum spring guns. This includes steel-core pellets with plastic casings. Once again, the danger is piston slap. Lightweight pellets are useful in lower-powered spring rifles and pistols but can be harmful (and inaccurate) when used in magnum spring guns.

Never use steel shot (i.e., BBs) in a rifled barrel. Airgun rifling is more shallow than firearm rifling in order to minimize velocity-robbing friction. Additionally, the metal used in airgun barrels tends to be "softer" than the hardened metal used in high-pressure firearms barrels. Steel shot will eventually strip the rifling of an airgun's barrel, even in guns designed to use both BBs and pellets. Lead BBs are available, but many of the guns designed for BBs are repeaters employing magnetic bolt tips that won't pick up lead BBs.

Do not "overcock" a spring gun. Most spring guns, whether barrelcockers, sidecockers, or underlevers, produce a distinct click when the sear "catches" at the end of the cocking stroke. Forcing the mechanism beyond that point can cause unnecessary wear.

Never leave a spring gun cocked for extended periods. This could weaken or break the spring. What is meant by an "extended period?" Leaving it cocked for an hour or two while hunting should not prove harmful to a properly designed and manufactured spring; any longer could be risky.

Never use penetrating oils, household oils, or firearm lubricants (i.e., any petroleum-based lubricant) in the compression chamber of an airgun. These low-flash-point oils could be detonated as the piston superheats the air during compression. The resulting explosion, or dieseling, can be harmful to both gun and shooter. Airgun manufacturers and distributors provide an array of lubricants suitable for the varied components of an airgun. These are readily available online or from airgun shops.

Never use a metal cleaning rod or bristle brush in an airgun barrel. This could damage the shallow rifling used in airguns.

See the section on barrel cleaning and lubrication for the proper method. Stuck pellets or debris should be tapped out using a suitably-sized *wooden* rod and mallet.

Compression Chamber Lubrication

The compression chamber houses the piston and piston seal and may be considered the forward area of the spring cylinder. Here the piston compresses the air that flows through the vent hole to propel the pellet. This chamber must be lubricated to reduce friction and ensure the effectiveness of the piston seal. Most modern piston seals are made of synthetics that require less frequent lubrication than the leather seals used in vintage and some current chinese guns. However, both types of seal must be lubricated to prevent power-robbing air blowby.

Lubricant: Sporter spring guns should use only a high-flash-point, silicone-based chamber oil to avoid dieseling. RWS sells suitable chamber oils. Recoilless match guns require higher-grade oils, so-called "Ultra" airgun lubricants.

Frequency: In sporter airguns with synthetic seals, 2 or 3 drops every 5000 shots should suffice (i.e., after shooting ten 500-round tins of pellets). Guns with leather seals should get a couple of drops of chamber lube every 1000 shots. Recoilless match guns should get two drops every 6000 rounds.

Procedure: In guns that may be uncocked manually (i.e., those that do not have an anti-bear-trap device) cock the piston and engage the safety. Attach a flexible oiling needle to the tip of the oil bottle. Keeping fingers away from trigger, insert needle through the vent hole and into the compression chamber. Squeeze out 2 or 3 drops of oil. Do not squeeze out a few more drops "just to be sure." Now cock and uncock the gun by grasping the cocking lever firmly, pulling the trigger, and allowing the lever to slowly return to its uncocked position. This should be done several times while tilting the gun at various angles to distribute the oil. In guns that can't be uncocked, as with guns fitted with an "anti-bear-trap" device, the gun should cocked, given a couple of drops of oil, then tilted for several minutes at various angles to effect oil distribution. The gun should be left in each position for several minutes. Guns with leather seals should be left uncocked and unfired for 24 hours to allow the oil to soak into the leather. The owners of tap-loading guns that do not permit direct access to the vent hole should open the tap, put in a couple of drops of oil, close the tap, then point the gun upward and cock the spring, drawing the oil into the chamber. The gun should then be tilted at various angles for several minutes to promote distribution. If the gun must be fired to uncock it, be sure to load a pellet before discharging it.

Compression Chamber Cleaning

Accumulated oils and grease in the compression chamber can cause low velocities or excessive dieseling. This condition is the result of overzealous lubrication or attempts by the manufacturer to protect the gun's innards from rust during potentially long shelf times. Although it is best to have a competent airgunsmith dismantle, clean, and lubricate such a gun, much of the oil and grease can dissolved and drained away by using molybdenum disulphide ("moly") in a liquid, evaporative carrier. Moly is useful in lubricating other components of an airgun and is sold under various names by several manufacturers. This procedure both cleans and lubricates the compression chamber, although it should be followed up by application of chamber oil to provide proper piston-sealing. The fine moly particles are carried by the liquid suspension into the crevices between mating surfaces where they fill the microscopic depressions in the metal. The carrier eventually evaporates, or is allowed to drain away as in this procedure, leaving behind a dry, superslick surface.

This procedure is similar to the one previously described in *Compression Chamber Lubrication*. The can is shaken prior to use and several drops of the liquid are introduced into the compression chamber via oiling needle. The moly liquid is distributed to all areas of the chamber by tilting the gun in various directions and working the piston back and forth (if the design permits). The gun must then be left standing, uncocked, on its muzzle over newspapers for several hours to allow the loosened oils to drain from the chamber and the carrier to evaporate. After draining, the chamber should be treated with chamber oil.

Cocking Linkage Lubrication. Cocking linkages are the moving parts that transmit the force of the cocking lever (whether barrel, underlever, or sidelever) to the spring during the cocking stroke. This includes pins, bushings, detents, pivot points, cocking rods, etc. These can be determined by looking for moving, metal-on-metal components as the gun is cocked. Some can only be seen with the stock removed. Some are easily visible simply because the metal is shiny where the parts rub against one another. All require lubrication to preclude undue wear and ensure smooth, quiet cocking of the gun.

Lubricant: Molybdenum disulphide (moly) in a liquid, evaporative carrier is an excellent lubricant for these components. The tiny moly particles are carried by the liquid suspension into the crevices between components and fill the microscopic depressions in the metal's surface. The suspension eventually evaporates, leaving behind a dry, superslick surface. Any lubricating grease formulated for high-wear components is also acceptable, if enough of it can be worked deep into the bearing surfaces. A thick motor oil is a much better lubricant than household oils, which are generally too thin to cling to the metal surfaces.

Frequency: Every 500 rounds or whenever the bearing surfaces appear dry.

Procedure: When using moly, place the gun over newspaper or rags to catch staining drips. Shake the can vigorously to ensure good particle dispersion in the carrier liquid. Put a couple of drops in the crevices between the metal-on-metal components. If possible, work the action slightly to draw the liquid into the mechanism. Wipe away excess surface

liquid. When using other oils, apply a couple of drops to the bearing surfaces and either work the action or tilt the gun to promote penetration of the oil. When using grease, be sure that it works its way into the component and does not merely gather on the surface. If it fails to penetrate, choose lighter weight grease or switch to motor oil or moly.

Spring Lubrication

Lubricating the powerplant of a spring gun reduces vibration during firing and will reduce friction between the spring and the cylinder wall or spring guides. Manufacturers typically coat their springs with a heavy grease for both rust protection and vibration reduction. Although excess grease on a mainspring can reduce velocity, it is neither necessary or advisable to remove all of it. Much of the grease is eventually flung from the spring coils over time, necessitating re-lubrication. The spring lubrication procedure described herein applies to sporter, not match, spring guns. The recoilless power mechanism of a match spring gun requires very infrequent lubrication and should be carried out only by a qualified airgunsmith.

Lubricant: Airgun retailers market oils specially formulated for use on the springs of sporter airguns and are typically labeled "spring oil." They also sell so-called "spring-dampening" compounds or gels. These thicker greases are applied to replacement springs, or degreased springs, in airguns undergoing overhaul.

Frequency: Every 2500 to 3000 rounds.

Procedure: Remove the stock, if necessary, to reveal the coils of the spring. Apply 3 or 4 drops of oil directly to the coils, evenly spaced. The oil will migrate over the surfaces of the coils during use.

Trigger Lubrication. In its simplest form, a trigger is a lever that moves the sear out of engagement with the cocked spring, thereby releasing it. In practice, this is no minor feat. The sear is under extreme tension while restraining the spring, so considerable force must be applied to trip it. The more complex triggers use compound lever systems to reduce that effort, or "lighten the pull." Although a smooth, clean-breaking trigger is more a function of design than lubrication, many triggers can be improved considerably with proper lubrication. The difficulty lies in identifying and accessing the surfaces requiring lubrication. Removal of the stock, followed by an examination of all visible trigger components as they move through their appointed paths, may reveal the surfaces that require lubrication. The more complex adjustable triggers may require further dismantling, a task best left to an airgunsmith.

Lubricant: Use conventional oils, molybdenum disulphide, or the "metal-to-metal" pastes marketed by airgun retailers.

Procedure: This varies with design and the degree of dismantling the owner is willing to attempt. If the bearing surfaces are made accessible, the paste or oil can be applied directly to them. In other cases, a couple of drops may be applied to outer surfaces of the trigger, then allowed to "seep" into the inner recesses of the mechanism, usually with the gun upended for gravity assistance.

Barrel Cleaning and Lubrication

The focus here is on removal of foreign materials (usually oil-based), followed by the depositing of a thin film of rust-preventing oil. The bore of a spring gun gradually collects debris flung from the compression chamber. This material - excess chamber oils, migrating spring grease, dieseling soot, etc. - can collect in the rifling grooves over time and degrade accuracy and velocity. The greatest deposits occur after compression chamber lubrication and with the initial shots from a new gun. Since leading is rarely a problem with spring guns (the shallow rifling and modest velocities usually won't strip lead from passing pellets), the metal cleaning rods, bristle brushes, and lead-dissolving solvents used on firearms aren't necessary and could harm airgun seals and rifling. Metal cleaning rods touted for use in airgun barrels should be also be avoided due to the potential damage they can cause to

rifling if improperly used. Flexible nylon cleaning "snakes," which are essentially strings that drag cloth patches through the bore, won't damage the barrel and can be purchased from airgun and firearms retailers. They can also be fashioned from a length of 50-pound test monofilament fishing line, as described in the procedure section below. Cloth patches are sold by the bagful in various "calibers," with .22 generally being the smallest available. These are easily trimmed for use in .177 barrels. Airgun retailers often have .177 through .25 patches, as well as felt cleaning "pellets" that can be soaked with cleaner or oil and pushed (never fired) through the bore.

Although a spring gun barrel should be lubricated regularly to prevent rust, bore cleaning is only necessary when accuracy or velocity degrades, or when visual inspection of the bore reveals the presence of debris. Some guns can go many thousands of shots before bore cleaning is required.

Cleaner: Use any "cleaner/degreaser" marketed by airgun retailers. Other degreasers may be used if kept away from breech seals, out of the compression chamber, and removed completely from the bore after cleaning. Do not use abrasive bore-cleaning pastes on shallow airgun rifling unless, as a last resort, it's needed to remove rust.

Lubricant: Retailers market a wide variety of rust-preventing oils for use in steel barrels. All will protect the bore of an airgun from rust if applied properly.

Procedure: Send the cleaning "snake" down the barrel from either breech or muzzle, attach a patch soaked in cleaner, then pull it back slowly through the bore. A tight fit is necessary. Discard the dirty patch and repeat the procedure until one emerges unsoiled. Pull a dry patch through the bore to remove traces of degreaser, then moisten a final patch with oil and drag it through the bore to protect against rust. When using monofilament fishing line, cut a piece several inches longer than twice the barrel length, send it down the bore, double it back to form a small loop to hold the patch, then push the remaining line back up the bore again; attach a patch to the loop and pull it up through the bore.

Rust Prevention. Steel surfaces, even if blued, are subject to rust and corrosion. They require protection from moisture and salts deposited by contact with human skin. Springers experience more skin-to-metal contact than other guns, but can be kept looking new with simple, regular care.

Wiping down all steel surfaces with an oily rag, then storing the gun in a dry environment, is effective, but oil can evaporate or migrate over time, leaving the metal unprotected. There are many products formulated to protect guns against rust and handling damage. Most are not traditional oils, but moisture-displacing chemicals that "plate" metal surfaces, leaving a dry, protective film. These can be found in any sporting goods store but work only if applied properly (some require a couple of initial applications). Also effective are the silicone-impregnated cloths used to wipe down the gun while camping or before casing it for the road trip home. Some breakbarrel spring gun owners use pure carnauba car wax (with no cleaning agents) or paste furniture wax on the exterior surfaces of their guns. This protects the surface from both moisture and handling wear.

The CO₂ Gun

CO_2 As A Propellant

Carbon dioxide (CO_2) is a non-toxic, non-flammable compound that occurs as a solid (dry ice), a liquid, and a gas. Happily for airgunners, when liquid CO_2 is confined in a reservoir, such as a CO_2 cartridge or bulk-fill tank, some of it converts to gas to fill the empty space. This gas exerts approximately 900 pounds per square inch (psi) pressure at 75 degrees Fahrenheit (°F). In CO_2 guns, this high-pressure gas is released a shot at a time to propel projectiles.

As the gas is released with each shot, some of the remaining CO_2 liquid instantly converts to gas and refills the emptied space. Each newly-converted quantity of

pressure will drop with each shot, as will the velocity of each pellet.

Temperature sensitivity is a disadvantage of CO_2, which gains or loses power as ambient temperatures fluctuate. The table below shows how temperature affects pressure. Although certain sophisticated CO_2 guns have valves that can compensate for temperature variations[3], CO_2 guns are primarily summertime or indoor shooters.

CO_2 Pressure (psi) Increase Relative to Temp. (°F)										
Temp	40	45	50	55	60	65	70	75	80	85	90
Press	560	590	650	690	750	790	850	890	950	1010	1090

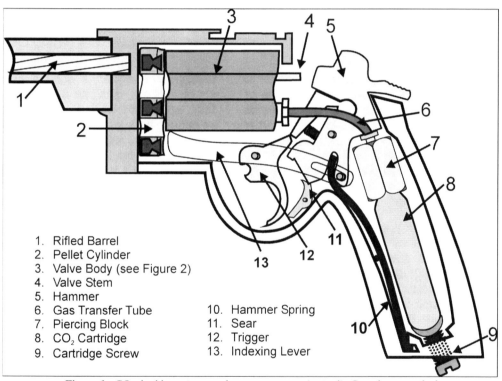

1. Rifled Barrel
2. Pellet Cylinder
3. Valve Body (see Figure 2)
4. Valve Stem
5. Hammer
6. Gas Transfer Tube
7. Piercing Block
8. CO_2 Cartridge
9. Cartridge Screw
10. Hammer Spring
11. Sear
12. Trigger
13. Indexing Lever

Figure 1. CO_2 double action revolver components (typical). Gun shown cocked.

CO_2 gas exerts that same pressure of 900 psi[2]. This consistency is maintained as long as liquid CO_2 remains in the reservoir. When no liquid remains, the gun will use whatever gas is left in the container, but the

Principal Components

The basic parts of a typical CO_2 gun are shown in Figures 1 and 2 and will be referenced throughout this section.

---

[2] CO_2 cools as it converts from liquid to gas; a rapidly fired CO_2 repeater will generate less pressure than a gun that is fired slowly, i.e., allowed to warm up between shots.

[3] These specialized valves will adjust to diminished pressure by remaining open longer during firing; this delivers a larger volume of gas for each shot and stabilizes the velocity.

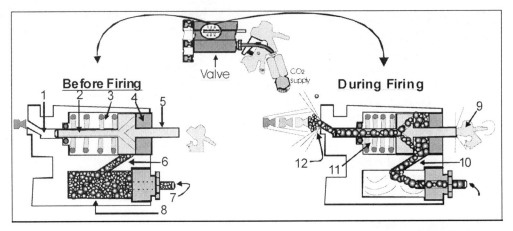

1. Exhaust Port
2. Valve Stem (hollow section)
3. Valve Return Spring
4. Valve Seat
5. Valve Stem (solid section)
6. CO_2 Passageway
7. CO_2 Inlet (from gas supply)
8. CO_2 Holding Chamber
9. Hammer Strikes Valve
10. CO_2 moves into Valve Stem
11. Return Spring Compresses
12. CO_2 Propels Pellet

Figure 2. CO_2 valve cutaway showing Valve Stem (5) before and during firing. Hollow section of Valve Stem (2) briefly opens the CO_2 Passageway (6) when Hammer (9) strikes the stem, allowing gas to flow to pellet. Valve Return Spring (3) instantly shuts valve for next shot. CO_2 Holding Chamber (8) refills with gas from cartridge.

In general, all CO_2 guns have a reservoir to hold the gas (i.e., a disposable cartridge or re-fillable tank); a valve fitted with an intake and exhaust port; a spring-loaded hammer that hits a valve stem to open the exhaust port; a trigger and sear to control the hammer; piping to route the gas to the projectile; and a barrel to direct the projectile to the target.

Although all CO_2 guns have similar firing components, they differ in how they store the CO_2 that powers the gun. Generally, there are two types of container for storing gas aboard a CO_2 gun: refillable (i.e., bulk-fill) tanks, and disposable cartridges. These systems are described individually in the sections that follow.

Bulk-Fill Tanks vs Disposable Cartridges

Refillable Bulk-Fill Tanks. The first CO_2 guns were produced in the late 1800s by the Frenchman, Paul Giffard, an accomplished inventor perhaps better known for creating the pneumatic tube for rapid mail delivery in office buildings. Giffard's 4.5-, 6-, and 8-mm guns used CO_2 tanks that unscrewed from the gun for refilling. The owner of such a gun would shoot until the tank ran out (after ~200 to 300 shots depending on power level selected), then exchange the tank for one that had been refilled at a service station. Although the guns were powerful, accurate, and exquisitely crafted, they never gained wide popularity, perhaps because of the difficulty of finding nearby cylinder exchange outlets for the then novel propellant. Later, around 1950, the Crosman Arms Company of Rochester, New York, resurrected the idea and began producing bulk-fill CO_2 rifles and pistols in addition to their respected line of pump pneumatic air guns. Produced in .177, .21, and .22 caliber, Crosman's CO_2 rifles and pistols had integral, non-detachable gas tubes that ran under the gun for nearly the entire length of the barrel. The tubes had threaded end caps through which the gun could be recharged from the large, cast iron bulk tank that was sold with each gun. The bulk tanks held 10 ounces of CO_2, enough for refilling the rifle or pistol several times before the tank itself had to be taken to a supply station for a refill, or to a Crosman dealer for exchange. Refills were a couple of dollars, but this purchased 800-2000 effortless shots, a boon to airgunners weary of pumping. It opened the doors to indoor match target shooting on a widespread

Schimel GP22 CO₂ Pistol. Rare and historically significant, the Schimel was the first CO_2 gun to use disposable CO_2 capsules (circa 1948). .22 caliber single shot; later models were 8-shot .22-caliber ball-shooting repeaters. 9.5-inch long; 5.75-inch; 2.5 lbs; windage adjustable rear sight; ~420 fps with 14.3-grain pellets; 20 shots per 8-gram seltzer bottle CO_2 capsule.

basis, something not practical with pump guns. Crosman developed and sold complete shooting range outfits[4] that could be set up quickly in corporate or school basements, and inter-company competitions became very popular, often being showcased in local newspapers. Crosman's original bulk-fill line-up consisted of the Model 111 .177 pistol, the Model 112 .22 pistol, the Model 113 .177 rifle, the Model 114 .22 rifle, and the Model 118 .22 repeating rifle. Later, 6-in. barreled pistols in .177 and .22 were added (Models 115 and 116). Although the guns sold well, there were complaints: refilling or exchange stations weren't always handy and the bulk-filling procedure, although not difficult, did

require education and attention, and was dangerous if done carelessly. This inspired Crosman to develop guns powered by disposable CO_2 cartridges that were easily loaded into the gun, an idea pioneered by the Schimel Arms Company of North Hollywood, California, in the late 1940s. The Schimel was a .22 single-shot pistol styled after the German Luger. It used readily available, 8-gram CO_2 bulbs used to carbonate water in seltzer bottles. Crosman's new pistols (Models 150 and 157, .22 and .177 cal.), debuted in 1954, but they used Crosman's proprietary 12.5-gram "Powerlets" instead of the smaller 8-gram bulbs.

CO₂ Bulk Filling Directions

The following directions apply to Crosman rifles and pistols produced from 1950 to 1954, but the principles apply to most CO_2 bulk-fill guns. They provide a general explanation of the basic procedures that are

---

[4] The outfits consisted of guns, targets, backstops, target retrieval systems, and stanchions to segregate shooters from the spectators. The guns were of an odd .21 caliber, forcing the user to buy Crosman pellets, and employed a supply tank that hung from the bottom of the gun just forward of the trigger guard.

Schimel backstrap was lowered and raised for both piercing the CO_2 cartridge in the grip and for metering gas for each shot. A tricky feature, the valve reset button (circled) had to be pressed for each shot before raising backstrap – or all gas in cartridge would escape instantly.

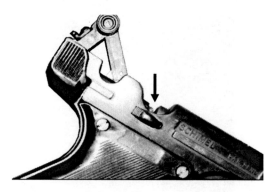

Schimel toggle had to be raised before each shot to reveal the pellet loading trough (arrow). Note the open rear sight fitted to the top of the back section of toggle. Subsequent manufacturer changed the rear sight to allow fitting the toggle with a magazine for 22 cal. balls. The in-line magazine used a spring to force each ball forward during the cocking/loading sequence. Manufacturing rights were transferred and gun appeared later under the names Carbojet and American Luger.

followed in filling the typical bulk-fill CO_2 gun, whether rifle or pistol, modern or vintage. There will be variations, of course, depending upon the manufacturer and the complexity and the sophistication of the design. It is always best to refer to the manufacturer's specific bulk-filling instructions, which are usually free and available online.

A few words of caution: CO_2 bulk-filling involves high-pressure tanks and a gas that can expand dangerously when heated. Tanks should be hydrotested to ensure they are safe for use. The tanks can be taken to a skindiving, paintball, or welding supply house for this service. CO_2 tanks, large or small, should not be stored in places where they can be heated beyond 100°F. Also, CO_2 tanks and onboard reservoirs must not be overfilled; this can occur when the supply tank is of a higher temperature than the gun or tank receiving the fill. An overfilled gun may explode if exposed to a warm room or hot car interior. To avoid this, safety-minded shooters use a scale for weighing the gun (or tank) before and after filling. It allows the shooter to know when the gun is safely filled, rather than dangerously overfilled. If the gun has a 3-oz CO_2 capacity, and the empty gun weighs 4 lbs, the filled gun must weigh no more than

4 lbs, 3 oz. If it does, the gun is overfilled. It may not fire if the hammer spring is not strong enough to overcome the unusually high pressure holding the valve closed, or it may be in danger of exploding if subsequently heated (especially if left in that hot car). An overfilled gun should be fired repeatedly to release the excess gas. If it can not be fired, the gun may be placed in a freezer for 15 minutes; this reduces the pressure of the CO_2 and should allow the hammer to operate the valve normally. If that doesn't work, the gun should be kept cool and taken to an airgunsmith for emptying.

Crosman Model 112 bulk-fill pistol produced from 1950 to 1954. Each gun was sold with a 10-oz, refillable CO_2 tank. 22 cal., 12 inches overall with 8-inch barrel; 2 lbs.; open, adj. sights; ~50 shots per fill; 510 fps with 14.3-gr pellets. A still-popular small-game getter among airgunning cognoscenti, the 112 is capable of sub-inch groups at 25 yds.

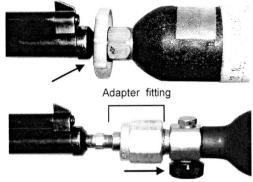

Bulk-filling Equipment: 1) Crosman original (circa 1949) 10-oz tank; 2) Model 112 pistol fill port and dust cap; 3) 3.5-oz tank; 4) 1/8-in. adaptor to allow use of 3.5- and 20-oz tanks; 5) 20-oz tank.

Bulk-filling a Crosman pistol directly from original tank (top) and from a paintball tank with adapter fitting. Both systems use On/Off wheels (arrows).

General CO_2 bulk-filling procedures are as follows:

1. Ensure gun is unloaded, then slide a wooden rod down the barrel until it reaches breech. CO_2 guns are notorious for pellets blown halfway up the bore by a nearly empty gas cartridge.

2. Put the gun on Safe.

3. Weigh the empty gun; record the weight.

4. Cock the gun. This ensures that the valve is closed, preventing gas from escaping during filling.

5. Unscrew dust cap covering the threaded filling head.

6. Screw the bulk cylinder into the filling head.

7. Position the gun so the tank is above the gun during filling. This allows CO_2 liquid, not CO_2 gas, to enter the gun. This is not necessary if the bulk tank is fitted with an internal siphon tube that draws liquid from the bottom of the tank. If CO_2 gas alone fills the gun, it will power only a few shots before the tank becomes empty.

8. Open the valve on the bulk cylinder. A slight hiss may be heard as liquid is transferred. Condensation may frost on the outside of the gun's gas reservoir as the cold liquid cools the metal.

9. After a few seconds, close the valve on the bulk cylinder.

10. Unscrew the bulk cylinder from the filling head. A loud hiss will be heard as the bulk cylinder is removed. This is the normal release of gas in the filling head and will stop after a moment.

11. Weigh the gun. Release gas (by shooting) if correct weight is exceeded.

12. Replace the dust cap on filling head. Gun is now charged and may be safely fired, stored, or transported.

12-gram CO_2 cartridges. Early style with crimped cap (top of illustration) was prone to leakage. Recent cartridges are shown at bottom. Empty cartridge at bottom left shows hole from gun's piercing pin.

Crosman's 160 single-shot CO₂ rifle. Bolt action; adj. trigger; aperture target sight; 39 inches; 5.5 lbs; 620 fps with 14.3 gr. pellets; one-inch groups at 30 yds. Gun uses two CO₂ cartridges, but can be bulk-filled via adapter cap. This superb gun has inspired multitudes of cheap, chinese imitations.

Some CO_2 guns can be bulk-filled or used with disposable cartridges interchangeably. This is typically accomplished by replacing the piercing cap used for cartridges with a separate screw-on cap that can take a fill from a bulk-fill tank. The cartridge chamber becomes, in effect, the gas reservoir. It generally does not hold as much CO_2 as a reservoir dedicated to bulk-filling, but such guns allow a hunter the option to head out with either a few gas cartridges or a bulk supply tank. It should be noted that some bulk tanks have a capacity as small as 3.5 ounces (equal to 99.225 grams, or nearly eight 12.5-gram cartridges) and can be pocketed easily.

Disposable CO₂ Cartridges.
Most CO_2 guns currently sold are powered by disposable 12-gram CO_2 cartridges. The cartridges can be bought for as little as fifty cents each and provide from 20 to 70 shots, depending upon the gun. Some vintage guns use the smaller 8-gram, seltzer-bottle cartridges. These are readily available online or from kitchen supply outlets or luggage stores, where they are sold for use in the seltzer bottles of portable "bars."

CO₂ Gun Operation
The guidelines provided here offer a general explanation of the basic procedures

that are followed in shooting virtually any CO_2 gun, whether rifle or pistol, current or vintage. There will be variations, of course, depending upon the manufacturer and the complexity and sophistication of the design. Refer to manufacturer's instructions, which are usually available free, online.

Charging. Charging is the process by which the CO_2 gas is made available to the gun. In most guns, the cartridge is placed in a pressure chamber fitted with a screw-cap. In other guns, usually pistols, it is placed in a yoke in the grip or under the barrel. Once seated, the cartridge must be forced against a piercing pin that will bore a hole in the cap and release the gas into the gun's internal components. The force is applied in various ways: by screwing the cap closed; by pushing a lever or button; or by a combination of both. Once the cap is penetrated, the high-pressure gas flows through the gun to a secondary chamber fitted with an exhaust valve. At this point, a dammed river of high-pressure gas extends from the cartridge to the valve. If all seals are operational throughout the gun, the gas will remain in place until the gun is fired.

It should be noted that some CO_2 rifles take two cartridges, back to back, in the pressure chamber. Such guns have two piercing pins, one in the bottom of the compression chamber and one in the screw-on cap. In these guns, the first cartridge is dropped nose-forward into the cylinder, the second is dropped in nose-rearward. The cap is then screwed on by hand (never with pliers) until tight, and then backed out a quarter turn, a step often omitted by neophytes. This pierces and releases the gas from one cartridge. The other cartridge is pierced by

Crosman 600, a true semi-automatic CO₂ pistol. 10-shot; .22 cal.; 10 in.; 2.5 lbs; adj. sights. ~325 fps with 14-gr pellets; 40 shots per cartridge; 1-in. groups at 10 yds. Manufactured 1960 to 1970.

Custom 12-inch-barrelled .22 CO_2 revolver (top) made from 4-inch-barrelled Crosman 38 Combat revolver (bottom). Custom gun is 17 inches overall, delivers ~550 fps with 14-grain pellets and 1-inch groups at 25 yds. Stock Crosman delivers ~350 fps with 1-inch groups at 10 yds. CO_2 cartridge is located in grip. Stock gun was originally designed for the US Air Force to simulate their government-issue Smith & Wesson .38 firearm, allowing airmen to familiarize themselves with their weapons in facilities without shooting ranges.

cocking and firing the gun.

Loading.
In single-shot designs, the shooter typically retracts a bolt, revealing a loading trough. He places a pellet nose-forward on the trough and closes the bolt, seating the pellet in the chamber. Repeaters require that a magazine of some type be filled with pellets or BBs. BB guns often have reservoirs that can hold a hundred BBs or more. Pellet revolvers have cylinders, sometimes removable, that offer multiple chambers, one for each pellet. Other designs use spring-loaded magazines that force a pellet or BB into the chamber each time the gun is cocked.

Cocking.
Cocking a CO_2 gun, whether single-shot or repeater, means retracting the hammer that will later open the valve and fire the gun. Hammers, which may be exposed or hidden within the gun, vary with design, but all are heavy, spring-loaded devices designed to strike the stem on the exhaust valve. Some hammers are thumbed back, like the hammer on a vintage six-shooter firearm; others are internal devices cocked by an external bolt or lever. In all designs, the hammer must be pulled back until it is caught and restrained by the trigger sear. This is usually signaled by an audible click as the sear engages a notch on the hammer. Some hammers have more than one sear engagement point. This permits the shooter to select the force of the hammer blow, allowing the gun to fire at either high or low power. Other guns have screws that adjust the tension of the hammer spring, which also allows shooting at varying velocities.

Firing.
Firing begins when pressure is applied to the trigger. As it is depressed, a system of levers begins to nudge the sear out of engagement with the hammer. When it's finally liberated, the hammer rushes forward and strikes the valve stem. The blow momentarily opens the exhaust valve, allowing a burst of gas to escape before the port is slammed shut again by the pressure inside the valve. The released gas travels through pipes and ports to the chamber where a projectile awaits. The gas drives the projectile down the barrel and out of the gun. The expanding CO_2 cools the gun slightly, an effect that increases with rapidity of fire. Any moisture present will condense in and on the gun as it cools. This condensation can cause rust, prompting some manufacturers to use non-ferrous materials in their barrels and pressure chambers.

Feinwerkbau C55 .177 cal. five - shot semi-automatic CO_2 pistol. Adj. trigger, sights, grips, and weight. Power supplied by 50-gram refillable canister. 7.5-in. barrel is vented to reduce muzzle flip in timed events. 2.5 lbs. 15 in.; 500 fps with 7-gr pellets. 0.20-in. groups at 30 feet.

It should be noted that CO_2 guns, unlike spring guns, fire almost without recoil, making them easier to shoot accurately and are a good choice for beginning shooters.

CO_2 Gun Variations

CO_2 guns store energy for multiple shots and are thus more readily adaptable to repeating mechanisms than spring guns. CO_2 guns have been produced as single- and double-action revolvers and as automatics and semi-automatics. The differences between these configurations are explained in the sections that follow.

Single-Shot. A single-shot is, essentially, a gun without a magazine. Pellets are loaded individually for each shot.

Repeater. Broadly, a repeater is any gun with a magazine. It includes all the types defined below.

Single-Action Revolver. A single-action revolver is a repeater with a cylindrical magazine that rotates and aligns a pellet with the barrel as an external hammer is cocked by the shooter's thumb. In this design, hammer cocking cannot be accomplished by pulling the trigger, as it can with the *double-action* revolver.

Double-Action Revolver. A repeater that rotates its cylinder, cocks its hammer, and fires as the shooter pulls the trigger. Many of these guns may be thumb-cocked before firing. This produces a much lighter trigger pull for letting off the shot, which usually results in more accurate shooting.

Semi-automatic. This is a repeater that, upon firing, siphons off some of the propellant to cock the hammer and chamber another pellet for the next shot. In this design, the shooter need only pull the trigger for each shot. True CO_2 semi-automatics are rare and expensive. Most CO_2 guns advertised as semi-automatics by marketers are, in fact, double-action revolvers that look like semi-automatics to the unknowing. Such guns are often styled to look exactly like popular semi-automatic firearms. The first true CO_2 semi-automatic pellet gun was the Crosman 600 pistol, produced in the 1960s.

Automatic. An automatic loads and fires projectiles as long as the trigger is held back and ammunition and power remain in the gun. This is popularly known as a *machinegun* or a *full-auto* weapon. Fully automatic BB and pellet guns are generally powered by air, since CO_2 guns cool, and lose power, when fired rapidly. Amusement park automatic BB guns are of this type, being fed by hose from large, hi-pressure air tanks. Some automatic airguns use multiple barrels rotated by an on-board electric motor. Automatic BB guns resembling .50 caliber Army machine guns were developed for training during WW II. The use of airguns (rifles, pistols, and full-auto) for training soldiers and police recruits was common in the US and other countries.

RWS 225 .177 cal. 8-shot CO_2 pistol. Mimicking a semi-automatic firearm, the 225 is actually a double-action revolver using a rotary magazine. The gas cartridge is located in grip. ~300 fps with 7-gr. pellet. Adj. sights. Offered with 4- or 6-inch barrels.

Benjamin Airsource 392 .22 rifle. Despite its name, the Airsource is powered by CO_2 from an 88-gram single-use, disposable cartridge that delivers ~250 shots at 600 fps with 14.3-gr. pellets. 39.5 inches overall; 5.5 lbs. Open sights adjustable for windage and elevation; grooved for scope.

CO_2 Gun Maintenance

Unlike pump pneumatics or springers, CO_2 guns do not have pump levers and pivot points that bear heavy mechanical and frictional loads, so there is very little in a CO_2 gun that can wear out in the conventional sense. In theory, they should last a long time and, in fact, many do. Some early Crosman bulk-fill guns have been known to operate continuously for decades without needing repair. Most CO_2 gun repairs involve the seals or O-rings that retain the gas, but seal failure is not an inevitability. It can be prevented (or at least postponed for a considerable time) if the owner lubricates, charges, and stores the gun properly. Preventive maintenance, therefore, should focus on those three areas.

Seal Lubrication. Proper lubrication will maintain seal functioning (sometimes for decades), and can occasionally restore a leaking seal. Put a single drop of Crosman Pellgun Oil or non-detergent 30-weight motor oil on the tip of every second or third CO_2 capsule before inserting it into the gun, or in the nozzle of the bulk-fill tank before screwing it into the charging port. The oil will be blown into the gun and migrate to all the internal seals. Some seals are readily accessible (such as the O-rings in piercing assemblies or screw caps) and may be lubricated directly with a single drop of oil when they appear dry.

Charging: Many CO_2 guns using gas cartridges rely on a screw-mechanism to drive the cartridge head into the piercing pin. With some guns, hissing will be heard as the cartridge is pierced, but it stops as tightening progresses. Stop tightening when

the hissing stops. Resist the temptation to over tighten this mechanism in the belief that it will ensure leak-free operation. Over tightening can distort or cut the O-ring.

Storage: Some guns should be stored charged with gas, others uncharged. Those that can be stored charged have a harder seal material than other CO_2 guns. As a general rule, vintage Crosmans of the '60s and early '70s used a harder material than later guns. The later Crosman models used a softer material that can be permeated, in time, by CO_2. The Smith and Wesson CO_2 pistols of the early '70s, as well as their current models, should be stored uncharged. Removing empty CO_2 cartridges is also a sensible precaution as they can adhere to the seals in piercing assemblies. In all cases, no charged gun or CO_2 cartridge should be left in direct sunlight or in a hot car or other environment that might experience temperatures in excess of 120°F.

Barrel Cleaning and Lubrication: As stated in the section on maintaining pump guns, compressed gases draw heat from their surroundings upon release. CO_2 guns also cool as they're fired, sometimes becoming frosty if fired rapidly in warm, moist conditions. Many of the vulnerable components are made of non-rusting alloys, but some CO_2 guns have steel barrels that will rust if condensed moisture remains within them. Although some of the oil applied when inserting the CO_2 cartridge will migrate to the bore and provide a degree of rust protection, wise owners will pass an occasional oil-dampened patch through the bore as added insurance, particularly if the gun will not be used for a time. A patch soaked with oil should be pulled through the barrel on a flexible barrel cleaning "snake" or tied to a length of 50-lb test monofilament fishing line. Cleaning the bore should rarely be necessary unless accuracy decreases. In such instances, a patch soaked with a cleaner/degreaser (marketed by airgun dealers) should be pulled through the barrel. Avoid metal cleaning rods, bristle brushes, and lead-dissolving solvents used on firearms. Do not use abrasive bore-cleaning pastes on shallow airgun rifling unless, as a last resort, it is needed to remove rust. Airgun and firearm retailers market a wide variety of rust-preventing oils for use in steel barrels. All will protect the bore of a CO_2 gun from rust if applied properly. Avoid "penetrating" oils as these can damage seal materials. Again, some guns have non-ferrous barrels (i.e., brass, as in early Crosman CO_2 guns and Sheridans) and need not be oiled. Hold a magnet to the barrel; if it sticks, the barrel can rust and needs to be protected.

Rust Prevention: All blued steel surfaces should have a thin film of oil, furniture paste wax, or chemical rust preventative applied after each use. Guns with brass barrels are usually painted or nickel-plated; such guns will require only an occasional wipe-down with a soft, non-scratching cloth.

Pump Pneumatics

Description

A pump pneumatic airgun, or *pump gun* as it is often called, uses an onboard system to compress and store the air that will eventually propel the projectile. It is this onboard pump that differentiates these guns from *pre-charged pneumatics*, discussed in the next section. Pre-charged pneumatics (PCPs) are either filled with air that has been previously pressurized and stored in a container separate from the gun (usually a SCUBA-type tank), or are filled with air pressurized by a pump separate from the gun (either a manual bicycle-type pump, or a mechanized compressor).

The pump gun's onboard pump uses a hinged lever positioned either under the barrel or alongside the receiver. Some early pump guns, as well as some current Asian models, use pump rods that extend from the front of the gun and are held down by the shooter's foot during pumping.

Pump guns usually require at least two or three strokes to bring the gun up to minimum operating pressure. Successive pumps increase the gun's power. Most pump guns are designed to exhaust all the air with each shot, although there are some that hold enough air for a subsequent shot or two, but at lower velocities. Pump guns are commercially produced in .175 (BB), .177, .20, and .22 calibers. Larger-caliber pump guns are available from small, custom airgun manufacturers. Some pump guns are designed to fire BBs and .177 pellets interchangeably. Pump pneumatic shotguns were produced by several manufacturers

Benjamin/Sheridan pneumatic .177 pistol. 12.25 in.; 2.5 lbs; 525 fps with 7.9-gr pellets at 8 pumps (max); brass barrel; adj. sights; walnut grips; sub-inch groups at 15 yds with scope; nickel-plated; pistol is also available in black paint and .22 caliber.

(Giffard, Plainsman, Vincent) but were not commercially successful. A current Crosman pump gun, discussed later in this section, has been used successfully as a short-range shotgun for taking pigeons, although it was not designed for such use.

Principal Components

The basic parts of a pump gun are shown, stylized, in Figure 1 and are referenced throughout this section. Figures 2 and 3 illustrate the position of the components during pumping (charging) and at the instant of firing.

All pump guns have a source of air, (i.e., the atmosphere), a valve fitted with an intake and exhaust port, a spring-loaded hammer to hit the valve stem, an air exhaust port, a trigger and sear to control the hammer, piping to route the air to the projectile, and a barrel to direct the projectile to the target.

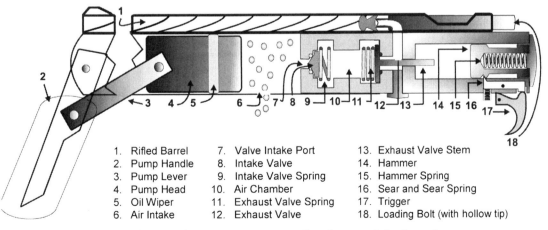

1. Rifled Barrel	7. Valve Intake Port	13. Exhaust Valve Stem
2. Pump Handle	8. Intake Valve	14. Hammer
3. Pump Lever	9. Intake Valve Spring	15. Hammer Spring
4. Pump Head	10. Air Chamber	16. Sear and Sear Spring
5. Oil Wiper	11. Exhaust Valve Spring	17. Trigger
6. Air Intake	12. Exhaust Valve	18. Loading Bolt (with hollow tip)

Figure 1. Typical pump gun components. Gun shown at air intake stroke.

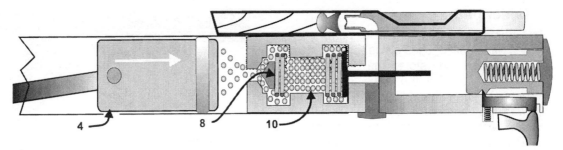

Figure 2. Compression Stroke. Pump head (#4) compresses air, opening the intake valve (#8). Air is forced into air chamber (#10). Intake valve is closed at end of stroke by pressurized air behind it. Subsequent strokes require greater force to open the intake valve, but will increase the power of the shot.

Operation

Charging. Charging a pump gun means forcing a large volume of air into a small, onboard reservoir, thus elevating the air pressure. The air is forced into the reservoir by a piston that moves back and forth in a tube (refer to Figure 2). The piston, which is operated by a sturdy pump lever, is fitted with a seal (oil wiper) that keeps the air ahead of it during the compression stroke. This compressed air forces open a spring-loaded intake valve, allowing the air to enter the air chamber.

After each stroke, the valve is snapped shut by the pressure behind it, retaining the air. The pressure within the chamber builds with each stroke, making it more difficult to open the intake valve with each successive stroke. This accounts for the difficulty of using a pump gun and explains why few shooters choose it as a plinking or target gun: unless the shooter is satisfied with the power from the initial two or three easy

pumps, the gun can be simply too tiring to use at full power over a lengthy shooting session. Pump guns are, however, popular with hunters, who need optimum power and fire relatively few shots in the course of a hunt.

One drawback of the pump pneumatic system is "air lock," a condition in which the hammer does not have sufficient force to open the valve to fire the pellet. This is usually the result of trying to increase power by pumping more strokes than recommended by the manufacturer. Certain pump guns preclude this by incorporating so-called "knock off" or "dump valves." This design does not rely on a spring-loaded hammer to open the valve; rather, the valve is closed at the first pump by a metal block that is later pushed open when the trigger is pulled. This mechanism prevents air lock, but results in a trigger pull weight that increases as the pressure in the valve increases. The advantages of the knock-off valve, however, have prompted some

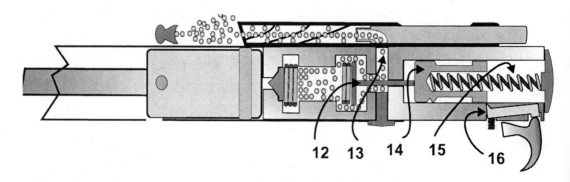

Figure 3. Firing Sequence. Trigger pushes sear (#16) away from hammer (#14), allowing spring (#15) to drive hammer against exhaust valve stem (#12), opening valve and letting compressed air into exhaust port (#13). Air enters hollow bolt tip and propels pellet.

Cannon 737 pneumatic .177 rifle. 34.5 inches; 4.5 lbs; carved wooden stock; brass barrel in plastic shroud; adjustable open rear sight; grooved for scope; hooded post front sight; 1000 fps with 7.9-grain pellets at 8 pumps (max); sub-inch groups at 40 yds. The short, lightweight scope was positioned to allow good grip for pumping.

manufacturers to develop sophisticated triggers that overcome this heavier pull.

Cocking/Loading.
Most pumpers that use pellets are single-shot weapons loaded in the same manner as CO_2 guns: the shooter pulls back (i.e., cocks) a spring-loaded bolt and places a pellet, nose forward, into a loading trough. Closing the bolt forces the pellet into the chamber. If the gun is a BB repeater, withdrawing the bolt allows its magnetized tip to pick up a BB from the reservoir, which is then carried into the breech when the bolt is closed. There are pellet-shooting pump repeaters with in-line magazine tubes. In these designs, the pellet is drawn into the loading trough by gravity or pushed into it by a spring. The pellet is then shoved into the breech when the bolt is closed. Whether single-shot or repeater, most pump pneumatics exhaust all air upon firing and have to be recharged for the next shot.

Note that some pump guns may need to be cocked prior to pumping, or the air will escape from the valve during pumping. For safety, pellet loading should be done after pumping, not before.

Firing.
Firing a pump pneumatic is essentially the same as firing a CO_2 gun. The firing sequence begins when pressure is applied to the trigger. In guns fitted with a spring-driven hammer, as the trigger moves rearward, a system of levers nudges the sear out of engagement with the hammer. The hammer finally breaks free and races forward to strike the valve stem. This opens the valve, allowing the compressed air to travel to the chamber where a projectile awaits. The high-pressure air drives the projectile down the barrel and out of the gun. In guns fitted with a knock-off or dump valve, the trigger moves the sear block, which allows the valve to blast open, releasing the compressed air.

Pump Gun Characteristics

A pump pneumatic is often the second gun purchased for a young shooter, following the venerable Daisy BB gun. Being recoilless, pump guns are easier to shoot than magnum spring guns, which usually require special holding techniques and considerable practice before they can be fired accurately. The pneumatic's lack of recoil also means that it won't damage scopes, making these guns suitable for use with optics that are not airgun-rated.

Pump pneumatics offer variable power: three strokes is usually sufficient for accurate, quiet, indoor shooting; additional pumps can supply power for small game hunting up to 50 yards or more, depending on the power of the gun. A pump gun's power will typically exceed the power of comparably-priced spring guns. The only monetary cost associated with pump guns, after purchase, is the price of the BBs or pellets.

Pump guns are generally short, light, and compact, attributes appreciated by hunters spending hours trekking through the woods. Since pneumatics remain essentially unaffected by temperature fluctuations, they'll perform the same on a winter rabbit hunt as on a hot summer ratting expedition. Most, however, require considerable time

41

Sheridan .20 cal pneumatic rifle. Similar version currently made by Benjamin/Sheridan in .177 and .22. Single shot; 37.5 in.; walnut stock; adj. sights; ~620 fps at 6 pumps (with Sheridan 16-gr. straight-walled pellet); 700 at 8 pumps (max); ½-inch, 5-shot groups at 50 ft.; shown with Sheridan clamp-on intermount and 4-power scope.

for reloading and recharging, and game animals won't wait around for the hunter to pump and load for a second shot. This seeming disadvantage, however, forces the shooter to learn the kill zones for the species being hunted, to stalk within range, and to make that first shot count.

Maintenance

Contrary to marketing claims, pump pneumatics are as durable as spring guns and will provide many years of trouble-free service if properly used and maintained. Most of the problems with these guns are caused by the owner's failure to lubricate the gun correctly, or to attempt to increase its power by overpumping.

Preventive Maintenance:

Do not overpump.

Manufacturers specify a maximum number of pumps for their guns (ex., 8 pumps for Benjamin/Sheridan; 10 for Crosman). Exceeding this limit will sometimes gain a few more feet per second of velocity, but will cause premature failure of the pump mechanism and can cause the afore-mentioned airlock. It is also possible to overpump a pneumatic without experiencing airlock; in this case, the gun will shoot, but a small amount of air remains in the gun after firing. This means that the shooter is wasting time and energy forcing those extra pumps. There is a safe way to determine if air remains in the gun after firing:

- *Without loading a pellet*, cock the gun.

- Place the muzzle near a small piece of paper on the ground.

- Fire the gun; if the paper moves, the gun is retaining air.

Residual air may be the result of a weak hammer spring, although it is more likely that the gun is being overpumped. If the spring is weak, it is a relatively simple matter to remove the old one and take it to a hardware store for a replacement. Yes, it is possible to insert a stronger spring, which might allow exceeding the maximum number of pumps without suffering airlock. This will, however, weaken the pump linkages and considerably shorten the gun's life expectancy.

Do not put oil in the air intake hole of the pump tube.

The oil will clog the valve, eventually causing air leakage. It could also make pumping excessively difficult, causing premature failure of pump components.

Do not "dry fire."

Do not cock the gun and "shoot" it without pumping it. The spring-driven hammer will strike the valve stem without the cushioning provided by air in the chamber. Unlike spring guns, however, a pump pneumatic may be safely pumped and fired without a pellet in the chamber.

Store properly.

Store the gun uncocked (and unloaded, of course) with a single pump of air to keep the valve closed and seals seated correctly. If the gun requires cocking prior to pumping,

Crosman 760 pump pneumatic rifle. Fires .177 pellets and .175 BBs; magazine holds 180 BBs; 35 inches; 4.5 lbs; rifled steel barrel; wooden stock; adj. sights; steel BBs penetrate ½-in pine board completely at 10 pumps; with lead pellets, the 760 can take small game to 25 yds. Magnetized bolt captures and holds BBs for firing; with repeated cocking, bolt will hold up to 6 BBs, allowing the 760 to be used as a shotgun for taking pigeons and doves on the wing to 20 yds. One of Crosman's bestsellers. Early model shown, introduced in 1966; current production models have plastic stocks.

uncock the hammer spring after pumping (to do this, tightly hold the bolt while pulling the trigger and slowly allow the bolt to return to uncocked position).

Pump Head Lubrication

The pump head must move freely in the pump tube, yet be tight enough against the tube wall to provide an effective air seal during pumping. The oil wiper permits this, but it must be lubricated properly, as follows:

Lubricant: Silicone oil.

Frequency: Every 300 shots.

Procedure: Open the pump handle, revealing a slot in the underside of the pump tube. Put two drops of oil in the slot behind the pump head and onto the tube wall. Do not put oil in front of the pump head or in the air intake hole. The oil should go behind the pump head and contact the wall of the tube. Subsequent pumping will distribute the oil throughout the tube.

Pump Linkages

There are typically three pivot points involved in transferring the energy of the pump stroke to the pump head. At each of these junctures will be a pin or bushing that bears the metal-to-metal load of each stroke, a load that increases with the number of strokes. Examining the pump mechanism while slowly opening and closing the handle will reveal these places. Regular lubrication at these points is critical to pump gun longevity. Lubricate as follows:

Lubricant: Use what the manufacturer recommends or silicone oil, molybdenum

disulphide (moly), or any lubricating grease formulated for high-wear components.

Frequency: Every 300 shots, or whenever the bearing surfaces appear dry or pumping becomes difficult.

Procedure: One or two drops at each pivot point. If using moly, shake can. Tilt gun to allow oil to flow into the component. Work the lever to ensure that oil penetrates into seams between components. When using grease, be sure that it works its way between the bearing surfaces and does not merely gather on the surface. If it fails to penetrate, choose a lighter weight grease or switch to motor oil or moly.

Trigger Lubrication

Most pump guns have triggers that use levers and linkages to restrain a hammer against a cocked hammer spring. On these guns, pulling the trigger pushes the sear out of engagement with a notch on the hammer, releasing it to drive forward and knock open the exhaust valve. Other guns have the aforementioned "knock off" valve that is opened directly by the trigger without the use of a hammer. Both types have metal-to-metal bearing surfaces requiring lubrication. Stock removal may be required to gain access to the surfaces. Lubricate as follows:

Lubricant: Use conventional oils, molybdenum disulphide, or the "metal-to-metal" pastes marketed by airgun retailers.

Procedure: This will vary with design and the degree of dismantling the owner is willing to attempt. If the bearing surfaces are accessible, the paste or oil can be applied directly to them. In other cases, a couple of drops may be applied to outer

XSB5-10 chinese multi-pump 10-shot repeating pistol with retractable shoulder stock. .177 cal; ~650 fps with 7.9 grain pellets at 8 pumps (max); 4.7 lbs; length 20 inches with stock retracted (shown); 30.5 with stock extended; open adj rear sight; ¼-inch groups at 15 yds.

surfaces of the trigger, then allowed to "seep" into the inner recesses of the mechanism, usually with the gun positioned for gravity assistance.

Barrel Cleaning and Lubrication

Compressed gases draw heat from their surroundings upon release. This cooling can cause moisture to condense in and on the barrel of a pump gun. The moisture will promote rust in a steel barrel unless the metal is protected by a moisture-displacing lubricant. Some manufacturers avoid the problem by using non-rusting brass or bronze barrels which require no oiling. Although a pump gun barrel is not subject to the burned oils and greases ejected from a spring gun compression chamber, it may still require occasional cleaning for optimal accuracy and power. Frequency of cleaning is indicated by a drop in accuracy or velocity or when barrel inspection reveals debris. Although regular lubrication after each shooting session is required to prevent rust, bore cleaning may not be necessary for many thousands of shots. Unlike firearms, airguns do not suffer from leading, an accumulation of lead in the barrel stripped from the sides of hi-velocity bullets, so the lead-dissolving solvents used with firearms should never be used.

Barrel Cleaner: Use any "cleaner/ degreaser" marketed by airgun retailers. Other degreasers may be used if the liquid is prevented from entering the exhaust valve (a ball of tissue or wad may be stuffed into the opening, which is usually visible at the bottom of the loading trough). Don't use abrasive bore-cleaning pastes on airgun rifling unless, as a last resort, it's needed to remove rust.

Barrel Lubricant: Retailers market a variety of rust-preventing oils for use in steel barrels. All will protect the bore of an airgun from rust if applied properly.

Procedure: Avoid using the metallic cleaning rods, bristle brushes, and lead-dissolving solvents used on firearms. Use only a flexible "snake," either bought from an airgun retailer or made from 50-lb test monofilament fishing line, as described in the section on spring gun maintenance. After each shooting session, send the snake down the bore, fasten a patch to the loop, moisten it with a couple of drops of oil, then pull it slowly through the barrel.

Rust Prevention

All steel surfaces should have a thin film of oil or chemical rust preventative applied after each use. Guns using brass barrels are usually painted or nickel-plated and require only a wipe-down with a clean cloth. Unless fitted with a handguard, the finish will likely degrade in the receiver area held by the shooter's hand during pumping. This can be prevented by occasionally buffing the area with hard automobile paste wax.

Pre-Charged Pneumatics

Description

A pre-charged pneumatic (PCP) uses air that has been compressed prior to being loaded into the gun. This compressed air is fed into an onboard storage reservoir from a bulk tank or directly from the air compressor (i.e., a pump). Pre-charged pneumatics were sometimes called SCUBA guns because they took their supply of compressed air from tanks used by underwater divers. This is still the most common method for filling a PCP, although there are now many variously-sized tanks designed specifically for PCP use. A SCUBA tank typically stores 80-cubic feet of air at pressures ranging from 3000 to 4500 psi. The great power of a PCP gun is understandable when one compares this

Once the onboard reservoir of a PCP gun is filled, the shooter need only cock, load, and fire the weapon until falling pellet velocities (or a pressure gauge fitted to the weapon) indicate the need for a refill. Most PCPs allow the user to adjust the velocity level; lower velocities not only increase the number of shots from a fill, but often produce the best accuracy. The reservoir on a PCP rifle can store enough air for up to 200 shots or more if the velocity is set at low level.

Pre-charged pneumatics are commercially available in .177, .22, and .25 calibers, but, because of their exceptional power, they are also produced in .30 and .45 calibers by custom airgunsmiths. Game animals that are too large for other airguns, such as

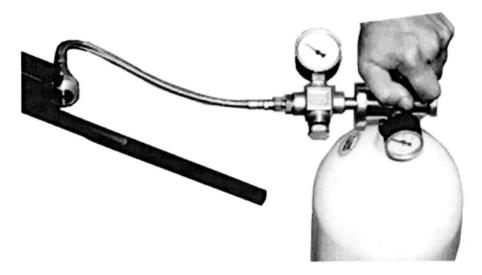

Filling a PCP rifle from a SCUBA tank. Hose is temporarily connected to the inlet port on the rifle (left) and is feeding high-pressure air from the SCUBA tank (right). Gauge in center indicates pressure inside gun and tells user when to close valve (under hand) to stop filling. Gauge on SCUBA tank indicates pressure remaining in supply tank.

pressure to the 900 psi of a CO_2 gun or the 1200 psi of a Sheridan pneumatic rifle.

Some PCP guns have no integral reservoir and use refillable changeout bottles that are screwed directly onto the gun, usually under the barrel in the forearm area. These "buddy" bottles are portable and easily replaced when empty, making them advantageous to field shooters. Such tanks can serve the same purpose as large SCUBA tanks and may be carried afield for filling guns that are fitted with integral reservoirs.

raccoon and javelina, can be taken with .30-caliber PCP guns.

Regulated vs Unregulated Guns

The pressure in the reservoir of a PCP gun diminishes as each shot is fired. As pressure decreases, so, too, does the velocity of each shot. This happens gradually; therefore, with any fill-up, there will be some shots with very high velocities (when the tank is full), some with very low velocities (when the reservoir is nearly empty), and some with moderate velocities.

Those with moderate velocity typically fall within a range acceptable to the shooter. For example, a gun may deliver a string of 30 shots (out of a total of, say, 70) that stay within ± 20 fps of 800 fps (i.e., 780 to 820 fps). The shooter may consider this an acceptable velocity range for the type of shooting he or she is doing. This grouping of shots with an acceptable degree of velocity variation is sometimes called "the heart of the fill" and it varies from gun to gun. In order to reduce velocity variation and increase the number of serviceable shots per fill, some manufacturers equip their guns with internal pressure regulators. A regulator is a secondary valve that can maintain a consistent output pressure relative to the primary firing valve despite

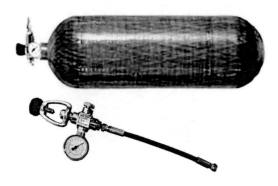

4500-psi carbon tank and fill adaptor. Adaptor connects tank to inlet port on gun reservoir. "D-clamp" on adaptor fastens to outlet valve on tank. Gauge indicates pressure as gun fills. Small wheel above gauge on adaptor hose opens bleeder valve to release air remaining in line after fill. Fitting at end of hose must match specific inlet port on gun.

the gradually decreasing pressure of the air in the reservoir. Many PCPs have a regulator as a standard feature, but regulators may also be bought through after-market airgun accessory suppliers.

Principal Components

Despite their much higher cost, many PCPs are as simple in design as CO_2 guns, pump pneumatics, and single-stroke pneumatics. However, they are built to withstand significantly higher pressures than other designs.

In general, the PCP has an onboard reservoir to store the pre-charged air, a

valve fitted with an intake and exhaust port, a spring-loaded hammer that hits a valve stem to briefly open the exhaust port, a trigger and sear to control the hammer, piping to route the air to the projectile, and a barrel to direct the projectile to the target. These components are illustrated in the sections on pump and CO_2 guns. The more-sophisticated PCPs may incorporate electronics that fire the gun, adjust power output, and alert the shooter to the status of the gun's energy and pellet supply. Such guns will usually incorporate the afore-mentioned regulator as well as an onboard pressure gauge.

Filling PCP Bulk Tanks. PCP bulk tanks are filled by the same type of gasoline- or electric-powered air compressors used to fill SCUBA tanks. Shooters may rely upon dive shops to refill their tanks[5], but individuals and shooting clubs often buy their own pumps. These pumps are fitted with pressure gauges, pressure relief valves, and moisture traps that ensure only dry air fills their tanks. They are also used to fill change-out bottles and buddy tanks, but the smaller volume of these tanks means that they may also be filled by hand pumps. These manual pumps resemble common bicycle tire pumps but are considerably more robust and generate much higher pressures. They are sometimes used to directly fill guns with onboard reservoirs, obviating the need for SCUBA tanks or access to a powered compressor.

Filling the PCP Gun. Guns that use changeout bottles are filled by screwing off the empty bottle and screwing on a full one. Guns with onboard reservoirs are filled by connecting the gun's filling nozzle to a supply tank and allowing the pressurized air to be delivered in a safe, controlled manner. The piece that connects the gun to the tank is called the filling adaptor. The filling adaptor is a length of high-pressure hose

---

[5] Dive shops may require a diver's certificate before filling a tank. The document certifies that the holder has been trained in the proper handling of SCUBA tanks, which can be lethal if mishandled.

Daystate Mk 3 Pre-Charged Pneumatic Rifle. Available in .177 and .22. Length 38.5 in; weight 7.5 lbs; adj. power 1 to 30 fpe; utilizes a rechargeable-battery-powered microchip that replaces the mechanical sear, hammer, and valve of traditional airguns. Electronic system adjusts power output and beeps to alert shooter of empty magazine and/or dwindling power supply.

equipped with a pressure gauge, an air-bleed screw, a fitting that mates to the SCUBA tank head, and a fitting that mates to the PCP's filling port.

Use manufacturer's manual for charging instructions. The charging instructions below are general guidelines.

1. Make sure that the gun is unloaded, cocked, and breech is open.

2. Briefly blast air out of the SCUBA tank to clear any debris from port and fittings.

3. Place D-shaped clamp over SCUBA valve and tighten with hand wheel.

4. Briefly blast air through adaptor to clear any debris. Screw free end onto gun's filling nozzle (or snap into place if using quick-connect fitting.

5. Close air-bleed screw.

6. Slowly turn hand wheel on SCUBA tank valve to release air.

7. Watch pressure gauge. If needle rises quickly, turn off SCUBA tank and start again even more slowly (fast filling will damage seals).

8. Turn off SCUBA tank valve when appropriate pressure is reached (see *Determining Optimal Pressure for an Unregulated PCP*, below). Never exceed manufacturer's recommended maximum.

9. Quickly open air-bleed screw to release pressure in adaptor.

When gauge needle drops to zero, remove adaptor from SCUBA tank and gun.

Determining Optimal Fill Pressure for an Unregulated PCP.

Optimal fill pressure is the pressure that delivers the most number of shots within a desired velocity range (for example, ± 20 fps of 850 fps). Many shooters are content to fill their guns to the manufacturer's recommend pressure and shoot until the velocity drops to an unacceptable level, but that will probably not yield the most number of useable shots, and it may not even provide the highest velocities of which the gun is capable. Some guns will actually deliver higher velocities when filled to a pressure lower than the recommended pressure[6]. Shooters who want maximum performance from a PCP gun will experiment with varying fill pressures to determine which one provides the highest number of usable shots. This exercise requires a chronograph and a calculator. A chronograph is a small, portable, battery-powered device for measuring pellet velocity. The chronograph measures the amount of time it takes for a pellet to pass over two separated light beams. An onboard computer in the chronograph converts that time to speed and displays the result in feet per second

---

[6] High-pressure air bearing down on the exhaust valve will allow it to stay open briefly when the hammer strikes it, allowing only a small volume of air to propel the pellet. A higher velocity may be achieved by a heavier hammer spring or decreasing the pressure in the valve, either of which allows the valve to stay open longer.

(or meters per second) on a liquid crystal diode (LCD) display.

To determine optimal fill pressure, the shooter fills the gun to a particular pressure and then shoots over a chronograph, recording the velocity of each shot. He then counts the number of shots that fell within a pre-determined acceptable range (for example, between 780 and 810 fps). The shooter may find that the gun delivers 35 acceptable shots at a pressure of 2700 psi, but 45 shots at a pressure of 2600 psi. He would then fill the gun to 2600 psi and "top it off" whenever it drops below that pressure.

Lubricating Pellets. Spring and CO_2 guns blow a certain amount of oil into the barrel with each shot. This tends to lubricate the barrel and reduce leading, the buildup of

Feinwerkbau C55P. Rapid fire, 5-shot semi-automatic target pistol; 15 in. length; 2.5 lbs; 510 fps with 7-gr. pellets; 200 shots per fill; on-board air pressure gauge at front alerts shooter of remaining power supply; adj. front and rear sights; adjustable Morini target grips.

lead stripped from pellets as they pass through the barrel[7]. This is not true of pre-charged pneumatics, which use unoiled air as a propellant (high-pressure air and oil form an explosive mixture). Leading can occur rapidly in these guns, adversely affecting accuracy. To avoid the problem, shooters oil their pellets. Oiling pellets is accomplished by dampening a folded cloth

---

[7] Leading is phenomenon that occurs primarily in firearms shooting unjacketed projectiles at high speed; most airguns, with their relatively low velocities, will never experience leading. PCP guns, however, can easily reach velocities where leading can occur.

FX 110-volt electric air compressor. Fills guns and SCUBA tanks to 3000 psi. 24 in. tall; 65 lbs. Liquid cooled, it can fill a SCUBA tank from 2000 to 3000 psi in 30 min. Features auto-shutoff at 3000 psi.

with the chosen lubricant (FP-10, Sheath, or a similar product) and rolling the pellets over it until they are coated. Another method is to put the cloth in the bottom of an empty pellet tin, soak it with lubricant, then roll the pellets inside until coated.

Loading. Single-shot PCPs typically incorporate a bolt and a loading trough into which the pellet is laid prior to being shoved into the bore by the bolt probe.

Removable 10-shot rotary magazine

Other single-shots have a breech that reveals the rear of the bore, allowing pellet insertion directly into the barrel. Repeaters may use a circular magazine similar to a revolver cylinder, although some of these require the shooter to cycle the cylinder by hand for each shot. Other repeaters feature a straight metal strip fitted with several pellet chambers. The bar ratchets a loaded chamber into alignment with the bore each time the bolt or lever is worked. Field shooters often carry several pre-loaded cylinders or strips for rapid changeouts.

Cocking.
Cocking a PCP means retracting and setting the spring-loaded hammer that will eventually strike the valve stem and fire the gun. This is accomplished by working a bolt or lever while loading the chamber.

Falcon FN8 PCP pistol. .22 single shot; 16.5 in.; 3 lbs; walnut grip; adj. sights removed for scope (grooved receiver); adj. trigger; adj. power; ~30 shots per fill at 600 fps with 14.3-gr. pellet for 12 fpe; up to 80 shots at 420 fps.

Firing Sequence.
Firing is essentially the same as firing a pump pneumatic. The sequence begins with finger pressure on the trigger. As the trigger moves rearward, a system of levers nudges the sear out of engagement with the hammer. The hammer snaps forward and strikes the valve stem. This blow opens the valve, allowing the compressed air to travel to the chamber where the pellet awaits. The high-pressure air drives the pellet down the barrel and out of the gun. Some advanced PCPs use electrically-powered mechanisms to accomplish these functions.

PCP Characteristics

PCPs offer substantially more power than spring, CO_2, or pumpers, making them suitable for short-range hunting of raccoon, woodchuck, nutria, fox, javelina, etc.

Many PCPs offer adjustable power, allowing them to be used for target shooting as well as hunting.

PCP power is not seriously affected by dropping temperatures. Unlike CO_2 guns, they can be used in the winter without suffering velocity loss.

Once the gun is charged, the shooter only has to load, cock, and shoot until recharging is necessary.

The air reservoir stores energy for a multitude of shots, making PCP guns viable candidates for repeating mechanisms, including semi- and full-automatics.

PCPs are generally much smaller and lighter than other sporting airguns, a considerable asset in field shooting.

PCPs, like other pneumatics and CO_2 arms, are recoilless, which means they're easier to shoot accurately and can be used with non-airgun-rated scopes.

PCPs are quite capable of handling the largest and heaviest "big-bore" projectiles (.25, and .30 caliber).

External power source means dependency upon tanks, refill shops, and/or manual, electric, or gas-powered pumps.

Manual pumps, if used as the primary re-fill source, require considerable effort; they are best used for "topping-off" a partially-filled tank.

Unsilenced PCPs are significantly louder than any other type of airgun, with noise that can exceed that of a .22 rimfire. However, many PCPs are manufactured with integral (i.e., legal) silencers that can reduce report to apartment-shooting levels.

PCPs require a regulated power source for optimal efficiency; this increases cost.

PCP are generally more expensive than spring or CO_2 guns.

Maintenance

It is usually best to follow the manufacturer's instructions for maintaining any airgun, but owner's manuals are not always available or complete. The following information should be considered as a general guideline. Be certain the gun is unloaded and uncocked before performing these or any maintenance procedures.

Storing. Store the gun with air in the reservoir. Storing it without air may allow rust to form in the reservoir, or cause the seals to harden. Pressure in the reservoir keeps the valve closed, preventing the entry of dirt or other contaminants.

Barrel. As stated, leading can occur in a PCP fired with unlubricated pellets. To clean the barrel, remove the bolt, then soak a brass bristle cleaning rod with alcohol (or any commercial leading removal product). Working from the breech end, run the brush back and forth through the barrel several times. Remove the brush and run a few dry cleaning patches through the barrel. When one patch finally emerges clean, soak a clean patch with oil and pass it through the barrel to prevent rust. This procedure should be repeated every 300 shots or whenever accuracy and/or velocity decreases.

Trigger Lubrication. PCPs are expensive airguns and generally have

Hand pump used for charging PCP guns and smaller, "buddy" tanks. Unsuitable for charging SCUBA tanks, it's similar to a bicycle pump, but generates much higher pressure. Pump is held in place by user's feet. Pumper uses upper body weight to assist in pump stroke, and flexes knees on up and down strokes. Hand pump is often sole source of pressurized air for PCP pistols. Most pumps are equipped with moisture traps and pressure gauges.

sophisticated triggers. Little maintenance should be required other than the application of light machine oil to bearing surfaces, applied without dismantling the mechanism. Should dirt, dust, or hardened grease inhibit smooth trigger functioning, a degreasing solvent should be used to clean the mechanism, followed by application of a light oil.

This may require a degree of disassembly beyond simple stock removal, and is best left to a competent airgunsmith. It may be possible to clean the mechanism, without disassembly, using pressurized solvents in a spray can. If disassembly is required, the intrepid and/or talented should secure an exploded drawing of the gun, and proceed slowly with proper gunsmithing tools. Digital photos taken at key points will aid in reassembling the mechanism.

Rust Prevention. After use, wipe all blued steel surfaces with a cloth dampened with rust preventative oil, taking care to keep the oil away from wooden stocks.

Single-Stroke Pneumatics

Description

Single-stroke pneumatics (SSPs) are powered by air that is compressed and stored by a single stroke of a pump lever. Unlike multi-pump pneumatics, SSPs do not have a valve that can hold increasing quantities of air. Of modest power compared to other systems, SSPs were originally developed as target guns because they provided recoilless shooting, consistent pellet velocity, and resistance to the temperature-induced velocity fluctuations experienced by CO_2 guns. The Walther LP2, predecessor to the LP3 (shown), was the first commercial use of this powerplant. The system is currently used to power inexpensive plinkers as well as expensive, Olympic-level target guns. The system has also been applied to sporting weapons, resulting in rifles generating nearly 12 fpe in .22 caliber. That level may seem feeble, but recall that the British are limited to 12 fpe by law and they routinely take small game with their airguns.

Principal Components

Single-stroke pneumatics use a piston within a tube to pressurize the air that drives the pellet. The piston is activated by an attached lever similar to the pumping lever used in multi-pump pneumatics. The SSP,

however, does not store multiple pumps of air. Attempting to put in a second stroke merely releases the air pressurized from the first stroke. The head of the SSP's piston, when it reaches the end of its stroke, forms one end of a chamber that contains the pressurized air. At the other end of the chamber is an outlet port. The SSP incorporates a trigger and sear mechanism that opens this port to release the air that propels the pellet. The port may be opened by a spring-loaded hammer that requires a separate cocking effort, or a "knock-off" valve that is "cocked" and ready as soon as the gun is pumped. Single-shot SSPs provide access to the breech for pellet insertion, usually a loading trough and bolt similar to those found on multi-pump pneumatics. Repeating SSPs have a reservoir for BBs, but load pellets singly.

Operation

Charging. Single-stroke pneumatics use a lever to move the piston within the compression tube (refer to overlay on figure of LP3). The location of the lever varies by design, but in practice they must all be extended to their farthest position, then returned to closed position, in order to compress the air. This requires force commensurate with the pressure achieved by a particular gun and may be more than

Walther LP3 .177 SSP Pistol. Length 13 in; weight 2 lbs 13 oz; microclick adj. rear sight; adj. trigger; ~380 fps with 7-grain pellets; ~0.06-in. 3-shot groups at 10 yds. Overlay shows piston in position after single charging stroke and the valve that will be knocked open by spring-loaded hammer. Inset shows pump lever open during the power stroke and barrel open for loading pellet directly into bore.

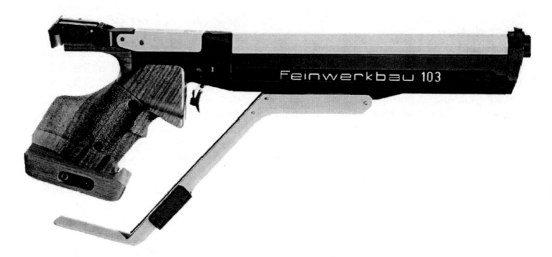

Feinwerkbau LP 103 .177 SSP Target Pistol. Length 16.3 in; weight 2.75 lbs; microclick adj. rear sight; interchangeable front sights; adj. trigger; adj. stock; ~500 fps with 6.9-gr pellets; ~0.02 3-shot groups at 10 yds. Removable pump handle also extends to increase leverage during pump stroke.

some shooters can tolerate over an extended shooting session. Some of the more sophisticated designs spread the charging effort between the opening and closing stroke. Others, like the Feinwerkbau LP103 (shown), provide an extendable lever to reduce the perceived effort of the charging stroke.

Loading. Loading procedures vary by design. Some guns use a bolt that must be withdrawn to reveal a loading trough; others use a cover or sliding panel. Once the loading area is accessed, the shooter places a pellet on the trough, or directly into the bore, then closes the bolt or cover. Transferring BBs from the reservoir into the breech is accomplished by working the bolt for each shot.

Cocking. An SSP typically has an internal spring-loaded hammer that must be cocked for each shot. In some designs, hammer cocking is accomplished automatically when the charging lever is activated, or it may require withdrawing a bolt or raising the cover over the loading port.

Firing. Firing is essentially the same as firing a pump gun. The shooter squeezes the trigger, which moves the sear out of engagement with the hammer. The hammer snaps forward and strikes the valve stem. This blow opens the exhaust valve, allowing the compressed air to travel to the breech and

blast the pellet down the barrel. In guns with "knock-off" valves, the block covering the exhaust port is moved aside by the trigger/sear mechanism, releasing the pressurized air.

Characteristics

- Recoilless shooting
- Consistent velocity
- Velocity unaffected by temperature
- Free power
- Compact dimensions compared to spring guns of the same power
- A charging stroke that can be difficult and tiring over extended shooting sessions, leading to muscle tremor during a match
- Low power relative to spring, CO_2, and pump pneumatics

The SSP in Hunting Use

As stated, SSP rifles generating nearly 12 fpe have been used effectively on small game at moderate ranges, but even low-powered SSP pistols have been taken afield. Knowledgeable shooters will often forego their more powerful spring pistols because they find it easier to put a pellet in the kill zone with an accurate, recoilless SSP pistol than with a bouncing, snapping springer. A pellet carrying 2.5 fpe to the skull

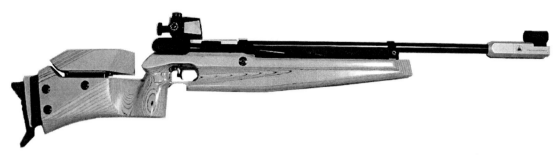

Feinwerkbau 603 SSP .177 Target Rifle. 10.7 lbs; 43.7 in.; 570 fps with 7-gr pellet; Olympic match accuracy (~0.04 in. groups); trigger pull 1 to 5 oz; adj. diopter rear sight, hooded front with interchangeable inserts; adj. stock; laminated stock resists distortion caused by humidity; barrel 16.7 in.; barrel sleeve 24.4 in.; short barrel reduces potential for shooter-induced movement.

of a rabbit will more surely drop the animal than a 6-fpe pellet in its gut. Not many spring pistol shooters can consistently hit a nickel at 30 to 40 feet, which is the level of marksmanship required of a humane, responsible hunter. Such precision, however, is routinely achieved by a practiced shooter using an SSP, particularly a hunter using one of the super-accurate target guns.

The single biggest drawback to hunting with an SSP is the fact that these guns can experience seal failure if left in a charged state for too long. Several minutes of pressure might not deform the piston head seal, but leaving the gun charged during a twenty-minute stalk, or during still hunting, could be harmful. The hunter could delay pumping until the quarry is sighted, but such movement, especially at the short ranges required by the SSP, will likely spook the animal.

Maintenance

It is best to follow the instructions provided with the gun. Some general maintenance guidelines are provided here.

Do not leave the gun in a charged state for longer than a few minutes. Do not pump until ready to shoot.

Bore: After every 300 shots, or when accuracy and velocity decrease, run a patch soaked with light oil through the barrel. Use a bore "snake" or a patch tied to fishing line, as described in the section on spring guns. No other type of bore treatment should be necessary as leading and accumulation of burnt oil does not occur in this type of gun.

Pump Lever. Examine the gun for the linkages and pins that operate the pump lever. These places where metal rubs metal bear the load of the pumping stroke and must be lubricated with moly paste or grease every 300 shots, or whenever they appear dry.

Compression Chamber. Open the bolt, loading port cover, or breech, and locate the air transfer hole that leads into the compression chamber. After every 500 shots, put 3 drops (no more) of 30-wt non-detergent motor oil into the hole and work the pump lever back and forth while holding the gun in various positions. This will distribute the oil uniformly within the chamber. If the transfer port (the passageway through which air travels to the pellet) is part of the bolt or cocking mechanism, it may be fitted with an o-ring seal that compresses when the bolt is closed. Use 30-wt oil on the seal and store the gun with

Marksman 2004 .177 pistol. 1.7 lbs; 9.5 in. long; rifled barrel: 4.5 in.; 385 fps with 8.5-gr pellet; sub-inch groups 33 ft.; plastic frame; steel barrel; upper part of gun pivots at front and is raised and lowered to compress air that powers the pellet.

Two British SSPs that achieved nearly 12 ft. lbs energy: Air Arms Genesis (top) and Parker Hale Dragon (bottom). Full-sized, accurate, and beautifully constructed, they provided recoilless shooting with power to take small game and are shown set up for scope use. Inset shows robust lever required to carry the charging load. That single pump stroke required considerable strength and shooting these guns could become tiresome. The guns did not sell well and are now collector's items.

the bolt open so the seal is not compressed; this will keep the seal supple and increase its service life.

Trigger. Removal of the stock or grip is often required to gain access to a trigger's bearing surfaces. Even then, further dismantling may be necessary. This should be left to a competent airgunsmith. Adventurous tinkerers should get exploded drawings and take photographs of the work as it proceeds; these will aid in re-assembly. Once the surfaces are revealed, lubricate according to manufacturer's recommendations, or apply a lightweight machine oil or moly paste to any metal-to-metal areas. The mechanism may be clogged with old lubricants and dirt. In this case, first degrease all components using alcohol or standard degreasers sold by airgun shops.

Simple, non-adjustable triggers can sometimes be lubricated without dismantling the gun. Turn the gun upside down and dispense a few drops of light machine oil into the crevices between the trigger blade and its housing, then allow the oil to "seep" into the inner recesses of the mechanism.

Rust Prevention. After use, wipe all blued steel surfaces with a cloth dampened with rust preventative oil. Consider applying a hard, non-abrasive car or furniture wax to metal surfaces exposed to handling. This will prevent sweat salts from attacking the metal. Guns using brass barrels require only a wipe-down with a clean cloth.

IZH-46 .177 SSP pistol. 2.5 lbs; 16.8 in. long; rifled barrel: 10.0 in.; 460 fps with 7.0-gr pellet; ~0.25 in. groups at 33 ft.; adj. sights and trigger aluminum receiver; steel air chamber.

Air Cartridge Guns

Description

An air cartridge gun is a pneumatic rifle, pistol, or shotgun that uses small, re-chargeable metal or plastic cylinders containing a projectile and a charge of high-pressure air. They look and operate like centerfire firearms in that the cartridges are simply loaded into the gun and fired. In fact, several air cartridge handguns are actual firearms converted by their man-ufacturers to use air cartridges. This creates a realism in appearance and function (if not in power and noise) that is much in demand by shooters forbidden by their country's govern-ment to own firearms.

The heart of this design is the air cartridge, a complex mechanism that may be considered a miniaturized version of the high-pressure air cylinder and valve used in pump pneumatics.

The air cartridge has a pellet-holding nose-cone that screws onto the body of the cartridge. Housed within the cartridge is the miniature valve and air chamber that permits air to enter during charging and to exit during firing.

Once fired, the air cartridge must be ejected from the gun, recharged with air, and reloaded with a pellet.

Currently unmanufactured, rifles and pistols designed to use these cartridges were available in .177 and .22 caliber. A .410 caliber shotgun was also available, as were pellet-firing air canes. The guns were sold with a special hand pump that refills the cartridges to a pressure of ~2250 psi with 5

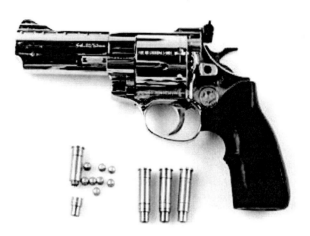

Brocock Orion .22 six-shot, double-action revolver. 2.5-in barrel; 7.9 in length; 2 lbs; ~380 fps with 12-gr pellets; adj. sights; rubber combat grips . Gun is, essentially, a high-quality firearm modified to fire pellets. Cartridge is disassembled, at left, for pellet loading and charging.

or 6 strokes. Adaptors allowed the cartridges to be filled by foot pump, an electric compressor, or a SCUBA tank.

Air cartridge guns were made in a variety of configurations but they were especially noted for guns resembling famous firearms pistols and rifles, both modern and vintage. These weapons were typically made to a very high standard and in many cases were virtually indistinguishable from their firearms counterparts. Various Italian replicators of American pioneer weapons adapted many of their guns to the air cartridge system. This includes the famous Colt 1873 Single Action Army revolver and the 1866 "Yellowboy" carbine. There was even a dead-ringer for the Walther PPK that uses slightly smaller air cartridges. The pistols were especially popular in countries where civilian ownership of firearm handguns is forbidden.

Of particular interest to hunters was the Saxby Palmer Ensign multi-shot, bolt-action .22 rifle. This gun used a large-capacity air cartridge that was charged by a heavy-duty, table-mounted pump. This gun fired pellets at nearly 800 fps.

Loading the Cartridge. The procedure is simple, but can be tedious

Air Cartridge cutaway showing screw-on nose cone containing pellet; center air chamber; central valve stem. Gun's hammer strikes "primer" in base to release the pressurized air. Cartridge is filled with air by a pump separate from the gun.

Saxby Palmer Ensign .22 bolt-action repeating rifle. Shown in original box with heavy-duty charging pump (for table mounting) and 10 air cartridges; 40 inches; ~6 lbs; adj. trigger and sights; grooved for scope; up to 800 fps, depending on number of pump strokes.

if the owner is preparing large quantities of cartridges: the shooter unscrews the empty

Captivating realism of air cartridge weapons has led to their being outlawed in certain countries, despite their non-firearm status.

nose cone, pushes the protruding exhaust valve back into the cartridge body, places the cartridge into the charger, pumps the cartridge with air (5 to 8 strokes), removes it from the charger, inserts a pellet into the nose cone, and screws the nose cone onto the cartridge body.

Firing Sequence. Air cartridge guns discharge in a manner similar to other pneumatic arms: when the trigger is pulled,

the sear releases its hold on a spring-loaded hammer located in the gun; the hammer surges forward and knocks open the exhaust valve stem in the "primer" area of the air cartridge; this releases the pressurized air that blasts the pellet out of the nose cone and into the bore of the gun. The difference between this gun and other pneumatics, is that the air chamber and exhaust valve are located in the air cartridge rather than in the gun.

Maintenance. Generally, the air cartridge gun will require less attention than the cartridge. The gun requires routine oiling of moving parts and the barrel, particularly if the gun will be unused for a time. The air cartridge, however, will perform best - and its seals will last longest - if the cartridge is frequently disassembled and its seals lubricated. As can be seen by the cartridge cutaway, the mechanism unscrews in two places, allowing access to the O-rings. These should be lubricated with oil recommended by the manufacturer, by Crosman pellet gun lube, or by 30-weight non-detergent motor oil. It is also important to seal longevity to limit the time the cartridge remains charged to no more than a day. Replacing seals is a relatively simple matter, however, and most owners of these guns will find a source of spare seals and keep a generous supply on-hand.

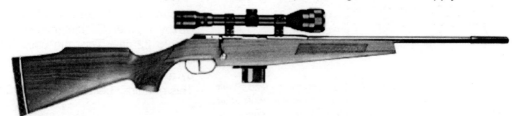

Brocock Predator 5-shot, .22 bolt action rifle. 38 in. length; adj. trigger; grooved for scope; walnut stock; match barrel; ~7 lbs; ~600 fps.

SIGHTING SYSTEMS

Introduction

A gun sight is an instrument that helps the shooter align the weapon more precisely with the target. Without sights, a gun can only be pointed, not aimed. Without sights, a gun's inherent accuracy won't be realized, no matter how fine the rifling, how smooth the trigger, how precise the pellet. The term system implies there are usually, but not always, two components acting in concert. The simplest sight is the bead atop the muzzle of a shotgun, which is not a system and allows little more than pointing. Although perfectly suited for establishing a lead on a hightailing mallard, something more precise is necessary for realizing the accuracy potential of a gun shooting a single projectile through a rifled barrel. For that reason, virtually every airgun leaving the factory is equipped with a set of sights[8]. But even these "factory" sights are often little more than adequate. They may allow the shooter to knock a beer can off a fence post at 35 yards, but the gun may be precise enough to hit bottle caps at that distance and such shooting often isn't possible with factory sights. It usually isn't long before the gun's owner considers an aftermarket upgrade. That's where the confusion begins.

Although there are many thousands of different sights available, making an intelligent choice need not be difficult. That bewildering array breaks down into a few basic categories. Once those categories are understood, the choice becomes far easier. It will quickly become apparent that certain systems are unsuited to certain types of shooting, or that some types of shooting can be successful only with a specific type of sight. This unit will examine each of the sighting systems available and provide representative samples of each. It should be understood that each type of sighting system has its place in the shooting world and that no one system is necessarily superior to another. Within each category, however, one example may be superior in design or construction to another, and the price will generally reflect that fact.

---

[8] *Many manufacturers of powerful, accurate air rifles sell their rifles without sights, knowing that the owners won't bother with anything but the finest optics.*

Open Sights

Description

Open sights, so called because they are *open* to ambient light, typically consist of a notch mounted at the rear of the gun over the receiver and a small post or bead at the front, or muzzle, of the gun. The shooter positions the gun until the front sight "sits" in the rear notch, then places the front sight just on, or just under, the target, whether the target is a tin can, bullseye, or the ear canal of a marauding rat.

Crude "fixed" (i.e., immoveable) rear sight (left) on vintage Hubertus pistol. This sight can't be adjusted, other than filing notch deeper to lower point of impact. Front bead sight (right) in dovetail mount can be hammered left (to move impact right) or right (to move impact left).

The front and rear components of this type of sighting system are manufactured in many shapes and combinations to suit their intended use. The front sight, for example, may be an open circle atop a post for surrounding a standard-sized bullseye in formal target shooting. The rear sight may be a wide, shallow "V" for gaining a quick, if coarse, sight picture. In some cases, the front sight may be hooded to reduce glare. No matter what the style, open sights require the alignment of three objects: the front sight, the rear sight, and the target.

The open sights supplied on most air guns are usually adjustable to some degree.

Sight picture when using Partridge style open sights: post front with square-notch rear.

Adjustability offers an important advantage over guns with immoveable, or *fixed*, sights.

A shooter may discover, for example, that his gun consistently shoots an inch left, though aimed dead center. He could compensate by aiming an inch right of the target, as he would if shooting in a right-to-left breeze, using so-called *Kentucky windage*, or he could make the gun shoot to point of aim by adjusting the rear sight slightly to the right. If the gun were grouping shots lower or higher than the point of aim, the sight could be moved higher or lower, respectively. Some front sights are also adjustable. The front sight is moved in a direction *opposite* the direction needed to change point of impact, i.e., the front sight is lowered in order to raise the point of impact.

Sheridan pistol open sights. Rear sight has small screw for elevation changes; large screw loosens, allowing entire sight to be moved left or right for windage adjustments. Ramp front sight is non-adjustable.

Adjustable open sights typically use screws for making windage and elevation adjustments, although less sophisticated sights will have a stepped riser for raising and lowering the rear sight. Some of the older European spring guns had rear sights driven solidly into dovetail mountings, providing an extremely rugged, compact unit. Windage adjustments were made by drifting them left or right with a hammer and punch. Elevation adjustments were made by aiming over or under the target, although the front sight could be filed down (to raise the point of impact). The process of sight adjustment is called *sighting-in* or *zeroing* and it is explained in detail in a later section of this book.

Sight picture when using bead front, U-notch rear open sights.

Advantages

- Simple, lightweight, and rugged. Less susceptible to damage during rigorous use than an aperture or optical sight.

- Aesthetically unobtrusive; unlike bulky telescopes, red dot sights, or laser sights, open sights will not mar the lines of a cleanly-styled airgun.

- Immune to heavy spring gun recoil, which can damage scopes that are not airgun-rated.

- Holds zero (i.e., position after sighting-in)

- Provides fast target acquisition, which means they can get on target quickly. Safari hunters use them when following wounded lions into the tall grass, as do airgunners snapshooting rabbits in the briars.

- Performs well in low-light situations, where an aperture sight or a scope might fail to acquire the target.

- Does not rely on delicate glass or battery-powered components (as do scopes, red dot sights, laser sights, and some scopes with lighted reticules).

Disadvantages

- Requires good eyesight for alternately focusing on three planes: front sight, rear sight, and target.

- Sight components can block out small targets, or targets that appear small because of distance.

- Generally too imprecise for taking full advantage of a gun's inherent accuracy potential.

Match sights on recoilless spring gun. Rear sight (above, left) has interchangeable inserts to change shape of notch; front sight (above, right) also has various inserts (below) that provide a variety of different sight pictures.

Sight picture when using bead front, V-notch rear open sights.

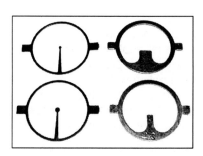

Aperture Sights

Description

Aperture sights consist of a front sight – usually a post or bead – and a rear sight that is a simple ring or hole in a metal disc. The shooter looks through this hole while aiming, giving rise to the name *peep* sight. The hole should be as close to the shooter's eye as possible, so peep sights are not generally used on pistols where eye relief (the distance between the shooter's eye and the sight), is too great. The aperture, therefore, is mounted at the rearmost point on the air rifle. Some target guns increase this distance by using mounting rails that position the sight over the grip of the stock. Some early 20th century air rifles mounted the aperture on the tang of the stock to bring it even closer to the shooter's eye.

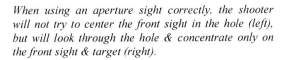

When using an aperture sight correctly, the shooter will not try to center the front sight in the hole (left), but will look through the hole & concentrate only on the front sight & target (right).

It is generally accepted that aperture sights will realize more of a particular rifle's accuracy than open sights. Shooters invariably print smaller groups when they upgrade from open sights to a peep. There are several reasons for this:

- Peep sights require the shooter to focus on only one object - the front sight - rather than the three required by open sights (i.e., rear sight, front sight, and target).

- The front sight and target are forced into sharper focus when viewed through the narrow aperture of a peep sight.

- The distance between front and rear sight is necessarily greater with a peep sight than with an open sight. This increased sight radius tends to minimize the effects of sighting errors.

- The peep sight is usually capable of more precise windage and elevation adjustment than an open sight.

Parker Hale aperture sight with target knobs. Top knob adjusts elevation; right knob adjusts windage. Indices on left and top keep track of each click. Large knurled ring provides interchangeability and shade for smaller interior peep.

Aperture sights are produced in a wide range of configurations. Although the rear component is basically a hole, it can be of various diameters: narrow for target shooting (~ 0.04 inch), wider for hunting (~ 0.05). Some apertures are adjustable, mimicking the iris of the human eye. Some are encircled by luminous rings for quick apprehension when hunting in low light. Others accept a lens ground to the shooter's prescription. Most apertures are screwed into the framework of the rear sight, making changeouts simple.

Front sights in this system exhibit even greater variation. Besides the plain bead, there are posts of various thickness, both straight-sided and pointed. There are rings used for bullseye target shooting, some of them sitting atop posts, others painted on clear plastic to appear free-floating. Serious peep sight users often choose a hooded front sight that not only reduces glare, but allows the use of interchangeable inserts. There are dozens of inexpensive inserts to match a wide range of shooting situations. There are also low-powered optical inserts (for both the front sight and the rear aperture), that clarify and/or magnify the sight picture. Front sight inserts are exchanged quickly and easily by simply loosening a locking collar, dropping in the replacement, and re-tightening the collar.

Sport aperture on scope rail of British spring gun. Knurled adjustment knobs replace flush screw heads to maintain settings under field conditions. Apertures of varying size may be used with this unit. Many airgun hunters prefer peep sights to scopes because of accuracy, lightness, ruggedness.

Target aperture sight on Steyr 10-meter Olympic-level airgun. Entire sight can be moved on rail for optimal positioning. Aperture diameter can be changed by twisting surrounding ring. Very precise windage and elevation changes are possible with this sight.

Virtually all of the aperture sights sold today are adjustable for windage and elevation. Inexpensive sights are moved laterally or vertically by sliding them within a framework fitted with a locking screw. The finer target and hunting apertures offer "click" adjustments that are made by turning knobs or screws. Each click moves the point of impact a specific amount, usually measured in fractions of a minute of angle (MOA), which is a measure of dispersion approximately equal to one inch at 100 yards. This means that a gun that shoots one minute of angle can be expected to group most shots within a one-inch area at

100 yards. Apertures for target shooting may have incremental adjustments as fine as 1/8-inch, which means that the point of impact will move approximately 1/8th of an inch at one hundred yards, or approximately 1/16 inch at 50 yards (a more realistic air rifle range). Apertures used for hunting have gradations larger than that. Most of the better peep sights provide witness marks painted or embossed on the rear sight, or on a plate fitted to the sight, that provide reference points while windage and elevation are adjusted.

Advantages

- Significantly better than open sights for realizing a particular gun's accuracy potential. Aesthetically unobtrusive; unlike bulky telescopes, red dot sights, or laser sights, aperture sights will not mar the lines of a cleanly-styled airgun.

- Two focal points rather than three, as required by open sights.

- Sporter models with screw adjustments are compact, rugged units that can hold zero despite rigorous use.

- Lighter than a scope, yet capable of offering much of the precision of a scope.

- Unaffected by harsh spring gun recoil that can damage scopes.

Globe front sight that accommodates various inserts for use with target rear aperture.

- Target models offer very precise click adjustments by simply turning a knob with finger pressure.

- Compact sporter models often enhance the aesthetics of a particular rifle. Even the larger target aperture systems lend an air of purposeful precision to the air weapon.

- Like open sights, they do not rely on delicate glass or battery powered components (as do red dot and laser sights).

Sport aperture sight with finger knobs for elevation (left knob) and windage (right knob) adjustments. Note the small set screws that "hold" the adjustment, once made. The center aperture can be unscrewed and replaced with an aperture of larger or smaller diameter.

Disadvantages

- Sporting apertures are difficult to use in low-light conditions. This can be offset somewhat by using a larger aperture or an aperture encircled by a ring of bright metal or luminous paint. Target apertures are of smaller diameter and admit even less light, but shooting matches are typically held in well-lighted venues with crisp black bullseyes contrasting sharply against white paper.

- Aperture systems can "overwhelm" small targets at longer ranges, particularly guns fitted with hooded front sights that hide or obscure the target.

- Mounting a rear peep and a hooded front sight often requires drilling and tapping, and that usually requires the services of an airgunsmith.

Scope Sights

Open sights (left) obscure part of quarry. Middle picture shows same image through 4-X scope. Image at right shows quarry through an 8-power scope. Scopes enable more precise (i.e., more humane) shot placement in hunting situations.

A scope on an airgun was once considered an extravagance, rather like a speedometer on a child's tricycle. However, as airguns advanced in power and accuracy, shooters realized that the full potential of these weapons couldn't be achieved with their simple, often crude, factory open sights. No, only a scope would get the most out of these guns, but in those early days, manufacturers weren't quick to see the advantages of optics on airguns. Although virtually all rimfires were advertised as "grooved for scope," most airguns lacked grooves, rails, or mounts. Determined owners had to have their airguns drilled and tapped for some form of aftermarket mount that would allow the use of a scope.

Today, however, virtually every air rifle, and many air pistols, come from the factory with some provision for mounting optics. And there are many custom mounts now available for vintage airguns that allow them to be scoped, releasing levels of inherent accuracy untapped when the guns were new.

Although scopes can be expensive, fragile, and disruptive of the smooth lines of a sleek airgun, many shooters won't use anything else. Some will pay more for the scope than the gun. So why is this system so special?

Advantages

For the average shooter, a scope makes it easier to hit the target - and at longer ranges - than with any other type of sight. Why? Because the target is no longer a hazy, indistinct object in the distance, but a big, bright image clearly visible in the scope. A scope is not a pair of front and rear sights that are alternately in and out of focus, but a crisp set of crosshairs virtually painted on the target. Since the target and the crosshairs are on the same focal plane, the eye can simply take in the whole scene at once, rather than try to focus on independent elements, some near, some far.

When one is accustomed to hunting with open sights, hunting with a scope for the first time can be startling. What formerly appeared over open sights to be little more

Sportsman Airguns QB-22 Deluxe CO$_2$ rifle with 6-power scope. Although this gun is capable of one-inch groups at 40 yds, such precision is difficult to achieve with stock open sights. High scope mount allows use of a scope with big, light-gathering, 40-mm objective lens. The scope mounts widen at base to form an opening that permits use of open sights for snap-shooting or close shots.

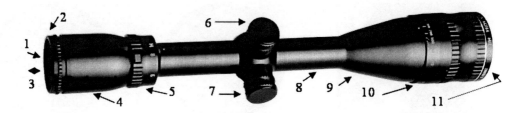

1.	Ocular lens	5.	Power Ring	9.	Objective bell
2.	Eye piece	6.	Elevation adjustment	10.	Adjustable objective
3.	Eye relief	7.	Windage adjustment	11.	Objective lens
4.	Eye bell	8.	Tube		

than a gray knot on a tree limb suddenly resolves into a squirrel's head – a *big* head, replete with glittering eyes and twitching nose. The crosshairs may tremble in a way iron sights never did, but this only serves to remind the shooter to settle down, to control the breathing, to smoothly squeeze the trigger.

Scope Terminology

Selecting the right scope from the myriad of types and styles available requires an understanding of terminology. The figure above provides the nomenclature for the components of a typical scope sight. The sections that follow provide an alphabetized glossary of other essential terms.

Adjustment Housing: The protruding section at the middle of the scope tube that contains the turrets for windage and elevation changes. It forms the juncture for the front and rear tube sections on scopes that do not have one-piece tubes.

Airgun Rated: Describes a scope capable of withstanding a spring gun's unique 2-way recoil. The scope will have strengthened lens and reticle mounts, or be constructed of materials resistant to spring gun forces.

Bell Housing: The front and rear housings for the objective and ocular lenses. Named after their appearance, although some scopes have straight tubes with a single-diameter throughout their length.

Caps: Removable covers that protect the front and rear lenses from rain, snow, etc. Some are made of a clear material so they can be used in-place, while hunting. Caps are also the removable covers (when so fitted) that protect the windage and elevation adjusters.

Clarity: The ability of scope to display target detail. Low-quality scopes will obscure details, or provide clarity only in the center of the lens.

Clicks: The incremental movements of the windage and elevation adjustors, often accompanied by a clicking sound. Each click will move the point of impact a set distance on the target, typically measured in fractions of an inch at 100 yards. The amount of movement is indicated on the adjustment wheel. For example, "1/4 inch at 100 yards" on the windage adjuster means that each click will move the point of impact 1/4 inch left or right on a target face 100 yards away. This corresponds to 1/8-inch movement at 50 yards and 1/16-inch movement at 25 yards. The same principle applies to the elevation adjuster for moving point of impact up or down.

Coatings: The material sometimes applied to the lenses to improve their light gathering and transmission ability. They are designed to prevent the reflection of light off the lenses.

Crosshairs: A pair of fine wires (originally hairs) intersecting at right angles inside the scope. They are used to align the scope with the target.

Elevation Adjustment: The mechanism that moves the reticle up or down to change the projectile's vertical point of impact on the target.

Eye Bell: The bell-shaped housing at the rear of the scope closest to the shooter's eye. It encloses the ocular lens and often provides an adjustment ring for focusing the reticle.

INSTALLING A SCOPE ON A GUN WITH GROOVES

1) Scope mounts will be attached to the grooves at top of receiver. Mounts can be positioned to provide optimal eye relief.

2) This set of mounts ("rings") comes with allen wrench for tightening bolts that hold ring halves together and clamp the mounts to the receiver.

3) "Jaws" at base of mounts clamp onto grooves. Scope should be laid in trough and mounts positioned before bolts are firmly tightened.

4) Top clamps are tightened slightly, at first. Owner should shoulder gun, peer through scope, and slide scope back and forth until image fills scope completely and crosshairs are horizontal. Only then are bolts tightened securely.

Eye Piece: The mounting for the ocular lens, which is the lens closest to the shooter's eye. Often this piece can be twisted in order to sharpen reticle focus.

Eye Relief: The distance between the shooter's eye and the scope's ocular lens at which the image in the scope is largest and in focus. Rifle scopes have approximately 4 inches of eye relief; pistols have about 15 inches.

Field of View: The amount of "real estate" captured in the scope's image, measured at a specific magnification and distance. For example, a 3X scope might display 33 feet (left to right) of the scenery when focused on a rabbit at 100 yards, whereas a 12X scope may show only 10 feet of that same area. The smaller the field of view, the more difficult it is to find the target, which explains why airgun hunters favor lower-powered scopes when pursuing moving targets. Field target airgunners, who are usually seated and have the time to fiddle with their equipment, tend to use higher-powered scopes in pursuit of their tiny, stationary quarry.

Fixed Objective: An objective lens that cannot be adjusted by the shooter to bring the target into focus. This means it cannot eliminate parallax error at varying ranges.

Fixed-Power Scope: A scope with one magnification level. Most fixed-power scopes are low powered (ex., 2X). See *variable* power.

Lens: The glass that is ground and coated to capture and transmit light. A scope has a system of internal and external lenses. The external lenses are the objective (front) and ocular (rear) lenses. The internal lenses invert and clarify the image, and incorporate the reticle. Changing the relationship between internal and external lenses changes the magnification and the point of impact.

Lighted Reticle: An illuminated reticle, typically crosshairs. The glowing lines are easier to discern when shooting at targets in a dark background. Illuminated reticles may be solar- or battery-powered.

Light-Gathering: The acceptance, and transmission, of light to the shooter's eye

INSTALLING A SCOPE ON A GUN WITHOUT GROOVES

1) *Mac-1-modified Benjamin/Sheridan .22 pump pistol. Develops 9 fpe at 14 pumps (550 fps with 14.3-gr pellets) for taking rabbits to ~35 yds. Scope is reasonable sight for this gun, but pistol is not grooved. Open rear sight is removed.*

2) *Two types of no-gunsmithing "intermounts" that provide grooves for scope rings. Solid intermount at left is vintage Sheridan item. Clamp intermounts at right allow more latitude in ring positioning.*

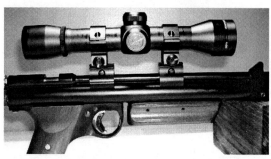

3) *Clamp intermounts fit over barrel and are held in place by cross-screws.*

4) *Scope rings attached to intermount; scope held in place by rings.*

by the scope's lenses. Light-gathering can often enable a shooter to see objects through a scope that would be unseen by the unaided eye. Effective light-gathering is important when shooting in low-light conditions.

Magnification: Sometimes called *power* and often written as a number followed by an X. Each increment of power makes the target appear an order of magnitude closer. A 4X scope will make a rabbit at 40 yds seem 10 yds away. There are 1X scopes that offer no magnification, but do provide a scope's light gathering, clarity, and focusing ease. Magnification has a downside: Scopes with high magnification (10X, 16X, etc.) will also seem to magnify the shooter's movements, producing jittery crosshairs. They also limit the field of view much more than low-powered scopes.

Mil-Dot Scopes: Originally used by the military, these scopes provide reticles with

multiple aiming points (seen as dots on the crosshairs) that are calibrated to specific horizontal and vertical distances. Depending on yardage and wind conditions, the shooter chooses a specific dot to place on the target. This eliminates the need to "aim high" for distant targets, or use "Kentucky windage" (aiming off-target left or right) to compensate for wind.

Objective Lens: The lens at the front of the scope that receives the light and is sometimes called the *bell*. Generally, the larger the objective, the greater the light gathering ability of the scope. The diameter of the objective lens is usually indicated in millimeters (mm). The larger objectives necessitate "high" scope mounts to allow the scope to clear the receiver or barrel. Objectives are either fixed or adjustable.

Ocular Lens: The lens at the rear of the scope, closest to the shooter's eye.

Parallax error: The apparent movement of the crosshairs across the target image when the shooter moves his head. The crosshairs must remain stationary when aimed at a target, despite any movement of the shooter's head. If they don't, misses will result even if the crosshairs appear to be on target at the moment of the shot. Parallax error is caused by the target image and the crosshairs being on separate focal planes. It becomes more pronounced as the scope magnification increases (it's relatively insignificant on scopes 4X and below). Firearm scopes are set at the factory to be parallax-free at around 100 yards, which is too far for most airgunning. Airgunners need scopes that will be in focus down to as little as 10-15 yards. The problem is corrected by setting the objective lens to the distance of the target, provided the scope has an adjustable objective. If it does have an adjustable objective, it's simply a matter of twisting the bell until the target image is sharply in focus. Scopes without adjustable objectives can be adjusted, although with some degree of difficulty (see *Eliminating Parallax Error in Fixed Objective Scopes* in this section).

Point of Aim: The place on the target at which the gun is pointed.

Point of Impact: The place on the target struck by the projectile. This is not always the point of aim.

Power: The magnification level of a particular scope, usually written as a number followed by X (a four-power scope is 4X).

Power Ring: The ring that increases or decreases the magnification of scopes with variable power.

Reticle: The aiming device within the scope that is positioned over the target image. In most scopes, this is a set of crosshairs, although there are numerous other configurations.

Rings: The circular pieces that hold the scope tube to the mount. Top half is removable to allow scope to be laid into the bottom half. Ring size must match diameter of scope tube (1-in; 3/8-in).

Seals: Rubber o-rings that keep moisture from entering the scope and fogging the lenses. Better scopes will have at least one seal at all potential moisture entry points, including front and rear lenses and the adjustment housing. Scope caps covering the windage and elevation adjustments should be secure (i.e., finger-tight) as these may be moisture entry points.

Tube: The metallic cylinder (usually aluminum alloy) that houses the lenses, their supporting mechanisms, the reticle, and the windage and elevation adjusters. For sealing purposes, a single-piece tube is preferred over a two-piece tube that is joined at the adjustment housing (turrets for windage and elevation adjustment). Tubes are typically 3/4-inch, 1-inch, or 30 mm in diameter; Generally, the larger the diameter of the tube, the greater the light gathering capability of the scope. The tube diameter determines the diameter of the rings required to attach the scope to the gun. Scope tubes are usually anodized; the more expensive scopes are hard-anodized and are significantly more resistant to scratches and wear than anodized tubes.

Turrets: The windage and elevation adjustment housings that slightly resemble the battle turrets on a castle. Scopes used for sporting purpose will have caps that seal out dust and moisture. These often require a screwdriver or coin for making adjustments once the cap is removed. Some target scopes have no caps; their adjusters can be turned by the shooter's fingers. The amount of adjustment in either type is indicated by index marks. Each incremental change is accompanied by audible, palpable clicks.

Variable Power Scope: A scope that offers several levels of magnification.

Windage Adjustment: The mechanism that allows movement of the reticle to the left or right to change projectile point of impact on the horizontal plane.

Mounting Considerations

Attaching a scope to a rifle or pistol requires a mount fastened to, or integral with, the gun, and a set of rings to hold the scope to the mount. The components must match;

not all rings will fit all mounts, nor will all scopes fit every set of rings. Specifically, the rings must have clamps that match the mount, and the rings must have a diameter that matches the diameter of the scope tube. The illustrations in this section show some of the different styles of mounts and rings available to meet an airgunner's needs. Of interest to vintage airgunners are those mounts that attach without the need for any drilling or tapping of the metal on their collector's item. An examination of one's gun (or manual) will reveal the type of mount required. This section describes certain challenges peculiar to airguns that may have to be met when mounting a scope.

Spring Gun Recoil Damage: As discussed in the *Spring Guns* section, spring guns have a unique two-way recoil that can damage the internals of a scope, even those scopes that can withstand magnum firearm recoil. Purchasers should contact the manufacturer of a prospective scope via their website to determine if a particular scope is airgun rated. This can also be determined by querying members of the many online airgun forums. A scope that is airgun-rated (i.e., spring-gun-rated) will be constructed of higher quality metals that will not deform, and ultimately fail, after repeated jolts. These scopes will be made of aluminum alloys approved for use in aircraft construction and this will be reflected in their price. Recoilless pneumatics and CO_2 guns do not require airgun-rated scopes, but they will certainly benefit from the lens quality and features (such as adjustable objective lenses) offered by the more costly scopes. Recoilless spring guns that do not use the sledge system (action riding on rails in the stock) for recoil elimination can also be fitted with non-airgun rated scopes. Guns that use the sledge system for recoil reduction transmit the recoil to the gun and scope, rather than to the shooter, and *do* require airgun-rated scopes.

Spring Gun "Scope Creep": This is the rearward migration of a scope mount in the scope grooves due to spring gun recoil. Frequently, no amount of screw-tightening or adhesives can thwart this slow advance,

necessitating the use of either stop-blocks or pins that engage holes in the mount or the rail.

Barrel Droop and Drooper Mounts: Some airgun manufacturers deliberately register a slight downward angle to the barrels of their breakbarrel spring guns to compensate for the comparatively low power and pronounced trajectory of airguns. This droop requires less elevation adjustment when using iron sights, but requires significant elevation adjustment when using a scope, in some cases more than is possible. This requires the airgunner to use shims, which can damage the scope, or use a drooper mount that incorporates a compensating degree of elevation adjustment. The shim material (such as a thin piece of aluminum cut from a soda can, or a snippet of 35mm camera film) can be placed between the rear scope mount ring and the scope tube before the ring is (very cautiously) tightened. Again, the use of a shim can damage the scope tube if the ring is over-tightened.

Scopes on Pump Rifles: Scopes are generally mounted over the receiver, the precise area on a pump gun that is grasped during pumping. It is possible to grasp the pistol grip area of the stock during pumping, but this is awkward. To solve the problem, some shooters use a shotgun scope positioned farther forward on the receiver. Shotgun scopes are designed to be used on slug guns during deer hunting and have a longer eye relief to keep the recoil from damaging the shooter's eye. Another solution is to mount a pistol scope (which has long eye relief) farther out on the barrel. It looks odd and can make the gun muzzle-heavy, but it works. Caution: Avoid over-tightening the screws on a mount that attaches to the barrel/pump tube unit; this could cause the barrel to separate from the tube.

Centering the Reticle

Getting maximum windage and elevation adjustment from a scope requires that the reticle start at the center of its adjustment range. This gives the user the maximum number of up-down, left-right clicks to get the gun sighted-in properly. Centering the scope's reticle is simple, but it can be tedious:

1. Turn windage adjustment to the left until it reaches the end of its travel. This will likely require cap removal and the use of a screwdriver or coin.

2. Turn the adjustment click-by-click to the right, counting each click.

3. Continue clicking and counting until the adjustment reaches the end of its travel.

4. Divide the final number by two. The result is the midpoint number for the windage adjustment.

5. Turn the adjustment to the left, counting each click, until the mid point number is reached.

6. Repeat steps 1 through 5 for the elevation adjustment.

Using a Scope as a Rangefinder

A high-magnification scope with an adjustable objective can double as a rangefinder. Many high-powered scopes have yardage indices stamped on the objective housing. The shooter twists a serrated ring on the front lens until the image is clear, then reads the yardage off the index. These indices may not always be accurate. The index may say, for example, that the target is 30 yds away, whereas actual measurement may be 28 yards. Most shooters will verify their scope's readings with a tape measure and re-mark the bell housing of the scope with the true readings. Being able to ascertain distances, and knowing the drop a pellet experiences at any given point in its trajectory, allows a shooter to hold over or under when aiming at a particular target (so called "Kentucky windage") or to adjust elevation and windage so the crosshairs can be placed directly on the target image. Accurate rangefinding is critical to success in field target shooting, which (currently) does not permit the use of rangefinding devices independent of the gun. The more expensive scopes will be capable of determining distances within one or two yards. Cheap scopes are incapable of this degree of precision.

Eliminating Parallax Error in Fixed Objective Scopes

It is possible for a determined airgunner (unafraid of voiding a warranty or destroying the sealing properties of the scope) to eliminate parallax error on a scope lacking an adjustable objective. The procedure will vary slightly from scope to scope, but the basic steps are the same:

1. Ensure that the gun is unloaded.

2. Center the crosshairs by following the instructions in this chapter. Off-center crosshairs can be a source of parallax error.

3. Place a small object at the distance to which the scope should be set to be parallax-free (25 yds is good for a scope used for airgunning small game).

4. Set the gun on a rest (folded towels on a picnic table works well).

5. Look through the scope and position the rifle so the crosshairs are on the target.

6. Without moving the rifle, move your head from side to side. If the crosshairs move off target, parallax error is present and must be corrected.

7. The goal now is to turn the front lens outward toward the target.

8. Examine the front bell housing. There will be a seam separating the bell housing from the main tube. It may be a narrow ring or a larger section. In either case, it has to be unscrewed. A solvent (acetone works) may be required to soften whatever sealant or glue was used by the manufacturer. Heating with a hair dryer may help.

9. When the ring is loose, unscrew it completely from the scope.

10. Examine the front lens. It will be fitted with a metal ring that allows it to be screwed in and out of the tube. The ring will have two opposing slots that permit it to be turned with a (improvised) spanner. It may also be possible to turn this ring by inserting a narrow-bladed screwdriver into one of the slots.

11. Turn the objective lens outward a quarter turn to correct parallax for shorter distances.

12. Look through the scope at the target and check for parallax reduction.

13. When the crosshairs no longer move off the target when you move your head, parallax has been corrected (for that distance).

14. Replace and tighten the locking ring.

Scopes on Airpistols

Although air pistols are used at ranges even shorter than air rifles, they, too, can benefit from a good scope. This is especially true of the high-powered pistols capable of taking small game. In pursuit of game, a scope increases the chance of putting the pellet in vital area, resulting in a "clean" kill. Some air pistols come from the factory grooved for scope use, others have enough metal on the receiver to have grooves cut into them. Still others can be drilled and tapped for the addition of a scope base. There are also clamp-on, no-gunsmithing bases available from a number of online airgun parts suppliers and airgunsmiths. Airgunners have been attaching scopes to air pistols for a number of years and they've solved most of the problems. It is generally not beyond the average airgunner's ability to affix a scope to an air pistol, and if it is, there are many competent airgunsmiths who routinely do it.

As stated, pistol scopes have longer eye relief than scopes for air rifles. It should be noted, however, that many shooters mount rifle scopes on their air pistols. This is not simply a matter of double-duty economy. Many shooters use detachable shoulder stocks on their pistols, making a shorter eye relief scope a necessity. Even those who don't use shoulder stocks appreciate the magnification, adjustability, and quality of a good rifle scope and will learn to hold the pistol close to the body to enable their use, despite appearances. The guiding principle is to use any sighting system that will enhance the effectiveness of the pistol, especially if it is used for hunting.

Selecting a Scope

There are many thousands of scopes available, so this section will not attempt to recommend specific brands or models. The following information provides a general guide to selecting a scope for each application. Proper scope selection should consider: cost; powerplant, and usage.

Cost: Cheap scopes may be tempting, and many of them are perfectly serviceable, but any airgunner who's experienced the precision, clarity, and 'feel' of an 800-dollar scope will never again be satisfied with the economy models. Indeed, some shooters simply can't win in high-level bench-rest and field target matches unless they use an extremely precise – i.e., expensive – scope. Even those shooters after tin cans or rabbits will admit that they really love the finer lenses and coatings of upscale optics, their machined tubes carved from billet aluminum, their windage and elevation adjustments that snick firmly into place, their ability to range-find down to a couple of yards. These are characteristics that simply can't be built into a cheap scope. So no matter what type of scope is selected, spending less usually means getting less.

Powerplant: As stated earlier, pneumatic, CO_2, and non-recoiling spring powerplants have no recoil or vibrations to damage a scope, so non-airgun-rated scopes can be used on them, and there are more of those available than airgun-rated scopes. Recoiling spring guns do require scopes with beefed-up internals, and these will be labeled "airgun-rated" by their manufac-turers. Note, however, that some scopes are labeled "airgun-rated" solely because they can focus down to airgun ranges, even though they may not have fortified mechanisms. The buyer is advised to research each prospective scope before purchasing it for a spring gun. Other shooters - not marketing hype - are a good source for real-world information on a particular scope and they can be readily contacted through online airgun forums.

Usage: Some scopes can do double or triple duty, being suitable for, say, hunting, plinking, and metallic silhouette, but there are some applications that demand a specialized scope. This section presents some of the things that should be considered when matching a scope to a particular application.

Hunting: Airgun hunters appreciate compact, lightweight scopes with good light-gathering capability and wide fields of view. Low magnification provides the field of view needed to spot and follow a bouncing bunny, but more magnification is often needed for smaller, distant quarry. A variable scope in the 2-7X or 3-9X range with an adjustable objective should be considered. Some scopes are offered with lighted reticles, making it easier to discern the crosshairs against dark backgrounds or twigs and brush.

Field Target: Field Target (detailed later in this book) involves shooting at metal replicas of typical airgun game animals at ranges out to 50 yards. The targets fall over if the shooter manages to hit, not the animal, but a paddle positioned behind a tiny hole in the animal's "kill zone."

These holes can be as small as 1/2 inch. Hitting such a tiny target requires the shooter to calculate yardage precisely, then adjust elevation and windage accordingly. A scope for this activity must be able to rangefind and must also possess precise, repeatable windage and elevation adjustments. Unlike hunters, high-level field target shooters will not "hold over" for the longer shots, or use Kentucky windage to compensate for breezes. They calculate how much a pellet will rise, fall, or drift at a particular distance, then adjust the scope's elevation and windage knobs the required number of clicks. This allows the crosshairs to be aimed directly at the kill zone. Scopes designed specifically for field target are generally long, heavy, complex, expensive, and – with their large sidewheels for focusing – not likely to be mistaken for any other type. Their high magnification (24X or more) and resulting jittery target image make them unsuitable for other types of shooting, except perhaps benchrest shooting, which demands similar scope attributes.

Red Dot Sights

Resembling a miniature scope, the red dot sight is an optical system of lenses and electronics in a tube that projects a tiny dot of light onto the target image (not the target itself, as does a laser sight). The shooter looks through the tube, aligns the gun until the dot is on the target image in the tube, and pulls the trigger. Unlike a scope, this system generally does not provide magnification. It is, essentially, 1X; an object at 20 yds will appear to be 20 yds away. This means there are no eye-relief considerations; so pistol and rifle shooters can use the same sight. Quick to get on target, these sights are favored by firearms practical-pistol shooting contestants, but have found wide use among airgunners.

Red Dot Sight Components

1) Cap covering battery chamber; 2) Light intensity adjustment knob (11 levels); 3) 30-mm ocular lens (1X power, no magnification; 4) Spare battery; 5) Mounting clamp screws; 6) Windage adjustment; 7) 30-mm objective lens; 8) Elevation adjustment.

Red Dot Sight Features

Power: Powered by tiny lithium batteries with approximately 15-hour non-stop usage duration. Electricity creates the small dot reticle that appears to float in the center of the target image.

Dot Intensity: Brightness of the dot can be adjusted by rheostat; the shooter turns a dial to increase or decrease the brightness to match ambient light conditions.

Dot Size: The size of the dot (adjustable on some models) is measured in minutes-of-angle (MOA); a 12-MOA dot will overlay approximately 12 inches of the target at 100 yards, 6 inches at 50 yards, 3 inches at 25 yards. A 3 MOA dot would cover 3/4 inch of target at 25 yards, far more suitable for an airgunner taking aim at a squirrel's head.

Systems are produced with dots from 3 to 16 MOA.

Tube Diameter: Tube diameter is measured in millimeters and the size contributes to both light gathering capability and field of view. A 30-mm tube could provide a field of view of about 68 feet at 100 yards, or about 17 feet at 25 yards. A 50-mm tube would provide a field of view of 22 ft at 25 yds and provide a higher level of bright-ness. Windage and elevation adjustments can be made by slotted screws covered by caps.

knurled

Mounting: Mounting requires the same rails or intermounts required for scopes.

Other Features: Higher-priced models offer dot-size adjustability, magnification, polarizing filters, and sun shades.

Sighting simplicity: With both eyes open, shooter places dot on target and squeezes trigger. Dot intensity can be changed to suit ambient light.

INSTALLING A RED DOT SIGHT ON A GUN WITH GROOVES

QB-1 folding-stock, bulk-fill, .177 CO_2 pistol. Rebarreled in .22; open rear sight removed; receiver drilled and tapped for scope base. Base positioned forward to allow loading/cocking trapdoor to open. Gun shown with aluminum adaptor to allow use of disposable gas cartridges.

Adaptors fasten to scope grooves and allow the red dot's Weaver-style base to be used. Lower clamps grasp the grooves and are tightened with allen wrench supplied with mounting blocks. Upper surface provides mounting surface for sight.

Adaptors fastened to grooved scope base. Indents in top of adaptor accept crossbars in red dot's base.

Red dot sight in place . Other red dot models have narrower tubes, but admit less light.

Although red dot sights are considered too imprecise for formal bullseye or field target shooting, they are well-suited for plinking, hunting, and casual target use. They are often chosen by those wanting to upgrade from factory iron sights, but need something more than a peep sight and less than a scope. Pistol shooters, who generally can't use a peep, especially like the compactness of a red dot compared to the size and weight of a scope. They may not get the target magnification of a scope, but they do get a light-gathering advantage as well as quick target acquisition.

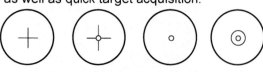

Some red dot sights offer multiple reticle styles with the turn of a dial.

Red dot sight shown with its windage and elevation adjustments exposed. The battery chamber cap has been removed. The system's 3-volt lithium battery is lying next to penny for scale. Battery can provide ~ 15 hours of continuous use. Most owners keep spares handy (~$2).

LASER SIGHTS

Picture this: You own a small place out in the country. It has a barn where the kids keep a couple of ponies, a miniature goat, and a goose. There's a family of rats residing in the barn, too. You're sure of it. You've seen the torn grain sacks, the droppings, those nasty bites on the ponies' fetlocks. At times, when you've slipped into the barn and stood in the gloom before turning on the lights, you've heard the squeakings and rustlings, and you've seen shadowy shapes moving along the base of dark walls. You've seen the occasional glint of . .what? Eyes? Teeth? You're loathe to use poisons around the animals, or traps

"You'll smack those rats in the dark with it," the dealer assures you. "Not pitch-dark, maybe, but close. As long as you can make out a shape, you can put the dot on it. Don't even have to aim. You can shoot from the hip … It's a pretty cool type of sight." And so you take it home, mount it on your pistol's trigger guard with its *fits-any-gun* mounting system, and sight it in on paper for 20 feet. For practice, you take some whiffle balls out to the lawn. Using a two-handed grip, holding the gun waist high, you have no trouble getting the dot onto the target, even in the bright sun. It's as easy as pointing your finger. You squeeze the trigger and *blam* – the

LASER SIGHT COMPONENTS

1. *Momentary pressure switch jack*
2. *Battery receptacle cover with hole for jack*
3. *Lithium battery receptacle*
4. *Momentary pressure switch jack connection*
5. *On/Off switch for continuous beam*
6. *Elevation adjustment (requires allen wrench)*
7. *Laser beam emission port*
8. *Momentary pressure switch button*
9. *Windage adjustment*
10. *Mounting clamp for grooved receivers*

around the kids. Yes, you've packed your trusty CO_2 pistol along a few times – the old Crosman .22 bulk-filler that'll put a .50 caliber exit hole in a bean can - but you can barely see the gun in your hand, much less the sights, and when you hit the lights, the rats disappear like smoke in a windstorm. . .

And then your airgun dealer suggests a laser sight. You've seen them in the case, but … aren't they for commandos with Berettas? Aren't they a bit much for an air pistol? Too complicated? Too… *electrical?*

whiffle ball leaps into the air. You laugh out loud. For the first time in your life you've hit a target dead-on without aiming – no shutting one eye, no lining up a front and rear sight, no squinting through a tube. Psyched, you drop a fresh wadcutter into the chamber, set the safety, and head for the barn …

Laser Sight Details

Operation: A laser sight incorporates advanced laser optics and microelectronics to generate a narrow beam of light with high visibility and low divergence (i.e., the beam doesn't widen much as it lengthens). They run on small lithium batteries, with most systems using two. An On-Off switch provides a continuous beam, or – for maximum stealth and battery life – activated as needed by a pressure switch velcroed to a handy spot near your trigger finger. Most inexpensive lasers use red light, while the more expensive use green – a color that can be seen more easily in bright sunlight or on bright targets.

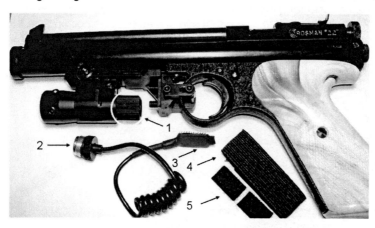

Laser sight mounted under barrel of Crosman single-shot, bulk-fill, CO₂ .22 pistol. Compact 9-inch gun weighs 1.2 lbs and fires 12-gr wadcutters at 500 fps with sub-inch groups at 30 feet. 1) screw-off cap housing constant On-Off button; 2) replacement cap for using momentary On-Off finger pad switch; 3) momentary switch with velcro backing 4) elastic band with velcro patch 5) stick-on velcro patches.

Mounting:
Some lasers sights provide "universal" mounts that can adapt to any air rifle or pistol. Others require a grooved receiver or a Weaver-style base. Some airgun manufacturers produce lasers designed to fit specific models of their guns and these are perhaps the easiest aftermarket lasers to mount. Still other laser sights are incorporated into the airpistol's design by the manufacturer, typically mounted in a rigid housing under, or alongside, the barrel. These guns integrate the pressure switch unobtrusively in the gun's grip. They offer the advantage of having iron sights available if the batteries quit.

Range:
Although originally intended for short-range tactical purposes, a laser sight could (theoretically) be used at any distance the dot can be seen (sunlight tends to "wash out" the dot), provided the gun is effective at that distance. However, most shooters typically confine laser sight use to 20 yds or less. The whole point of a laser sight is to have a very fast sight that can be used in near darkness. It is not intended for long-range shooting.

Sighting-In: With this system, sighting-in is the process of aligning the path of the laser with the path of the pellet (see chapter on sighting-in). Since the laser travels in a straight line and the pellet in an arc, the shooter must establish a place along the pellet's path where it intersects the path of the laser. That inter-section point should be the range at which the shooter expects to take most of his or her shots. Our rat hunter, for example, will be taking all of his shots at about 20 feet. To sight-in his gas gun, he set up a paper bullseye at 20 feet, and, using a rest to minimize shooter-induced movement, aimed the laser at the bullseye and fired three shots. He noted where the shots were grouping on the paper, then adjusted the windage and elevation controls on the sight until subsequent shots hit the bullseye. He then fired at shorter and longer distances and discovered that shots at ranges less than 20 feet hit *above* the dot, while shots beyond 20 feet hit *below* the dot.

Laser sights mounted directly under the barrel of a pistol or rifle can be given their preliminary sighting-in using the gun's open sights. Once the laser has been securely mounted, turn it on, point the gun at a blank wall across the room, then make windage and elevation adjustments on the laser sight until the red dot is sitting atop the front sight when the gun is aimed with the open sights.

And now let's get back to that barn full of thieving rats . . .

Crosman with momentary switch installed. Note the cap installed in back of laser, replacing the constant switch, and the finger pad velcroed to the elastic band on the grip. Middle finger rests on pad and depresses it only when laser is needed.

You approach the barn door quietly, but the ponies hear your footfall on the gravel. *Time to eat,* they think, and you hear shuffling and snuffling as they circle in their stalls. You slowly open the left-hand door just enough to slip inside, then slide the door closed. . .

Weak shafts of light slant in from the little windows over the stalls, but you see nothing at ground level – at first. As you wait for your eyes to adjust, you hear that tell-tale scratching and peeping. Yes, they're here in the semi-darkness, feeling safe because you haven't turned on the lights. And then your eyes adjust to the gloom and you discern that place across the floor where concrete floor meets wooden wall. . .

There's a lump down there, a black hunched thing, right at the base of the wall. You raise the pistol waist-high and hold it with both hands, nice and steady. The lump stays put. Your movement doesn't set the animal fleeing. He can't quite see you. To him, you're just a black shape against a dark wall. You tap the switch on the pistol and a tiny red dot appears on the wall 20 feet away.

The rat still doesn't move, even as you inch the dot down the wall. You know he's watching, waiting, unconcerned. The red dot starts to tremble, but you take a few deep, slow breaths, and the dot becomes steady again. Now the dot reaches the lump, fracturing as it hits the glossy hair, sparkling like cracked glass.

You begin to squeeze the trigger as you move the dot to the shoulder, now the neck, and, finally, the head. Then, just as the red bead hits that nearly bald patch between eye and ear, the sear releases the hammer. The little chunk of lead blasts out of the Crosman, spinning smoothly, zinging across the barn and smacking the rodent's skull with a loud crack. The bone shatters, caves in. Dead, the rat drops its head to the floor. This is just too easy, you think, as you quietly reload your pistol.

Laser sight on .20-caliber SSP 250 pistol. This 14-inch, 3 lb, multi-caliber handgun (.177, .20, .22) launches a 14.3-grain pellet at 510 fps at 75°F and is an excellent dim-light, short-range, rat and rabbit gun. Sporting a forestock, the gun can be pointed with precision. A laser may be the best sight system for introducing beginners to the fun of shooting.

Holographic Sights

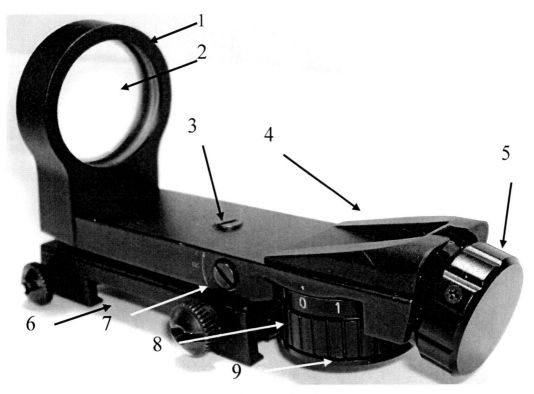

Holographic Sight Components

1) Lens frame; 2) Reflex lens; 3) Elevation adjustment screw; 4) Light-emitting diode and mirror housing; 5) Dot selector knob, provides a menu of dots and circles; 6) Mounting rail for Weaver-style mounts; 7) Windage adjustment screw; 8) On/Off switch and intensity control knob – provides 11 brightness settings; 9) Battery cover for 3-volt lithium battery.

The holographic sight is an electronic aiming system that evolved from the "head's up display" developed for U.S. fighter pilots. In this military application, an image of the jet's instrument panel is projected onto the jet's windscreen. This allows the pilot to monitor the status of his aircraft without taking his eyes off the scenery – which could include enemy fighters approaching at 1500 miles per hour.

In the civilian application, a light-emitting diode generates a reticle – typically a red dot or a crosshair – and projects it onto a small transparent panel in front of the shooter's eyes. In some of these sights, the hologram will appear to be projected in the air some distance in front of the weapon, but in most systems the dot or crosshair appears in the panel which is made of layers of shatterproof, scratch-resistant glass treated with anti-reflective coatings. The lens provides no magnification.

The holograph's speed advantage accrues in the civilian shooting application as in the military: the marksman can bring his gun to bear and take aim without removing his eyes from the target, whether it's a paper bullseye or a bounding rabbit. Because the shooter does not have to locate his quarry in a scope tube, or align it with a front and rear sight, the holographic sight is probably the fastest aiming device yet created.

Many holographic sights offer a selection of reticles. Some involve a large, thin-ringed outer circle with a tiny dot in the center. The large outer circle allows rapid target acquisition while the fine dot allows for more precise aiming, as time may permit. Additionally, as the sight is essentially parallax-free, eye alignment behind the sight is not critical. As long as the shooter can get the reticle on the target, no matter where it may appear in the lens, the target will be hit.

INSTALLING A HOLOGRAPHIC SIGHT

1) *Russian IZH-61 sidelever .177 spring rifle. Shown with its adjustable stamped steel open sight on grooved receiver. Electrified holographic sight will complement gun's futuristic styling.*

2) *Factory sight is held to gun by single screw under elevation wheel. BSA holographic sight, which requires Weaver-style mounts, cannot be attached directly to grooves. Adaptors are necessary.*

3) *Adaptors provide Weaver-style mounts and are held in place by cross-screws.*

4) *Holographic sight in position. It must now be sighted-in to match point of impact to point of aim.*

Holographic Sight Features

Power: Powered by 3-volt lithium battery with approximately 20-hour non-stop usage duration.

Dot Intensity: Brightness of the dot can be adjusted by rheostat; the shooter turns a dial to increase or decrease the brightness to match ambient lighting conditions.

Dot Size: The size of the dot is changeable on some holographic sights by turning a selector wheel imprinted with icons representing the various sizes. Dots are measured in minutes-of-angle (MOA); a 12-MOA dot will overlay approximately 12 inches of the target at 100 yards, 6 inches at 50 yards, 3 inches at 25 yards. A 3 MOA dot would cover 3/4 inch of target at 25 yards.

Mounting: Mounting requires the same rails or intermounts required by scopes.

Holographic sights permit fast target acquisition. Keeping both eyes open, the shooter locates the target in the frame, places the dot where he wants the pellet to land, and squeezes the trigger. The dot does not need to be in the center of the frame for accurate shot placement. In the image above, the holographic dot is shown between the squirrel's eyes.

SIGHTING-IN

Sighting-In, Defined

Sighting-in, or *zeroing*, is the process of adjusting an airgun's sights so that the point of aim (POA) is the same as the point of impact (POI). An airgun clamped in a vise will cluster pellets in one area of a paper target, but the gun's sights may not be "looking at," or aligned with, that same area. If that gun were taken afield, it would miss its mark every time, no matter how skilled the shooter.

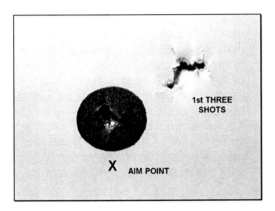

This target illustrates the reason for sighting-in, or zeroing, an airgun. The first 3 shots were fired from a rest, with the gun aimed at the base of the bullseye. The shots grouped at 1 o'clock, nearly an inch from the aim point. After windage and elevation adjustment, the fourth shot took the center out of the bull. Without zeroing, shooting sessions with this gun would have been a frustrating waste of pellets.

Sighting-in is an essential aspect of airgunning, whether the shooter is after tin cans, ten-rings, or junkyard rats. One simply cannot assume that a newly-acquired rifle or pistol, or one that's been left in a closet or car trunk for a few months, will shoot where it's aimed. Many perplexed shooters are heard to complain, after a well-executed shot missed the target, that "the sights must be off." They're probably right. The sights could indeed be "off." Many factors can change a gun's zero, ranging from a direct blow to the gun to the more subtle effect of a wooden stock swelling or contracting with changes in humidity. In fact, many shooters discover that merely taking off the stock or scope and putting them back on again, or tightening loose stock screws, or switching to another style or weight of pellet, will necessitate a re-zero of that particular gun.

Briefly, zeroing an airgun involves determining the POI at a specific distance (usually the distance at which most shots will be taken), with a single brand and weight of pellet (usually the one that has proven most accurate in that particular gun), then adjusting the sights so that the POA is aligned with the POI. Simple in concept, zeroing can be frustrating if not done in an orderly, organized manner. This section discusses the conditions and equipment needed to zero a gun and provides a step-by-step procedure.

Equipment, Conditions

The following equipment and conditions will prove helpful in zeroing an airgun:

A Sight. Obviously, the gun must be equipped with some sort of sight system, whether open, aperture, scope, red-dot, holographic, or laser. The principles in this chapter apply to all of them. Some sights are easier to adjust than others, requiring only the turning of a knob, while others will require a hammer and drift punch. Many scope and aperture sights provide graduated indices (i.e., little lines) printed on their adjustment controls. These indices, sometimes called "clicks" because of the sound they make when moved, correspond to movement in POI at a specific yardage. This information is often stamped on scope sight adjustment wheels. For example, "One click = ¼ inch" means that one click will move the POI ¼ inch at 100 yds. Other increments are provided in the table below.

Point of Impact Changes per "Click"

Increment	POI	POI	POI
"½ in at 100	1/8	1/4	1/2
"¼ in at 100	1/16	1/8	1/4
"1/8 in at 100	1/32	1/16	1/8

On some sights, the direction of POI movement may be indicated by a directional arrow with L or R (for left or right) on windage adjustments, and Up or Down on elevation adjustments.

Sighting-in is done from a rest. Some guns may group better without hand under forearm (below). Experimentation is required, as each gun is unique.

Time. Zeroing shouldn't be rushed. Setting aside a few minutes for sighting-in a gun the morning of a hunt is a mistake. It may take a good deal of time to establish exactly where the gun is shooting, then to adjust the sights.

A Wind-Free Day. Sighting-in involves determining where the gun – not the wind – sends the pellet. A steady left-to-right breeze, for example, could cause lightweight airgun pellets to drift an inch or more to the right at 25 yards. Adjusting the sights on such a day will have pellets landing off-target to the left on a windless day. The solution is to sight-in on an indoor range, or outdoors on a calm day.

A Gun Rest. While zeroing, the shooter must minimize any external forces that could move the gun during aiming and firing. Although it is possible to use a heavy machine rest to clamp a gun into immobility, this is neither practical or even desireable

for the average airgunner. Excellent results can be obtained by sitting at a table and resting the gun on bench-rest bags ("rabbit ears"), or a rolled-up towel or blanket. Airgunners in the field have used hay bales, tree stumps, truck tailgates, or lightweight folding shooting benches, all with some type of padding between the gun and the rest.

It is essential that spring guns, including recoilless guns, be isolated from any hard surface during shooting. Laying the forearm of a recoilling rifle directly on a hard surface will cause shots to scatter across the target, making zeroing impossible. It is usually best to lay the forestock of the rifle on the palm of the hand first, then settle the back of the hand down onto the soft rest. Guns vary, however. One gun may shoot tighter groups if it's held under the forearm, another may group better if laid directly on the rest without a hand under the forearm. This can only be discovered by experimentation.

A Target. Keep it simple. Tape a sheet of white, loose-leaf paper to a cardboard box. Using a coin and a black marker pen, draw a couple of bullseyes evenly spaced in the center of the page. Place the target box in front of a safe backstop at the distance most shots will be taken, or fill the box with tightly-packed rags. Set the box at the same height as the shooting bench. Instead of a box, a suitable target holder can be made from an inexpensive wire-framed For-Sale sign, or election sign, designed to be pressed into soft earth. There are paper sighting-in targets that provide multiple aimpoints superimposed on a measured grid. These tell the shooter precisely how far the POI is from the POA. As stated earlier, these distances correspond to the indices on most scope and aperture sights, eliminating the guesswork on how much to move the sight. There are also adhesive-backed paper targets that reveal hits by turning fluorescent green or orange at the pellet hole, allowing groups to be seen from the firing line. If sighting-in is done in the field, the shooter should be sure to bring thumbtacks or tape to affix the target to a tree or fence post. The target should be set at the same height as the rifle when positioned on the shooting bench.

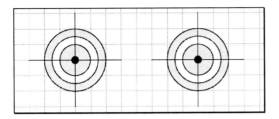

Sighting-In targets offer measured grids that show how far, in inches, the POI is from the POA. This helps to determine how many "clicks" to move the rear sight to align POI with POA.

The Sweet Spot. Some air rifles, particularly springers, "like" their forearms to be held in a certain place and manner if they are to shoot their best groups. One gun, for example, may shoot best when held far forward on the forearm, another may "prefer" a grip closer to the trigger guard. Also, one gun may prefer to be held gently at the wrist (i.e., the area behind the trigger), while another responds best when held firmly. Finding the sweet spot and the manner of holding that produces the best accuracy requires experimentation. The shooter will apply these findings scrupulously once the gun has been zeroed.

Slight changes in hand position and firmness of hold can improve accuracy. This is particularly true of spring guns. Experimentation is required.

When zeroing pistols, most shooters will use a two-hand grip and rest their forearms, not the butt of the pistol, on the rest.

Tape Measure and Notebook. Although a gun will be sighted-in, or zeroed, for one distance, it will be used on targets at varying distances. The shooter needs to know where the pellet will be (i.e., how far below or above line of sight) at different points in its arcing flight path (see Figure 1). This is best determined by simply shooting directly at bullseyes on paper targets set at varying ranges, usually at 5-yard increments, out to the maximum effective range of the gun, and observing where the pellets are hitting each target. Some pellets will hit a certain distance below the bullseye (when the targets are closest to the shooter), some will hit right into the bullseye (at the zeroed range), and some will hit a few inches below the bullseye (when the targets are farthest from the shooter).

There are ballistics tables and programs (available online) that can predict the position of a hypothetical pellet above or below the line of sight at specific yardages during its travel – if the pellet's weight, muzzle velocity, and ballistic coefficient are known. Although this would seem to preclude the need for actual shooting, such data may not correlate precisely to one's particular circumstances. Shooters requiring realistic information about pellet location at each yardage (i.e., hunters and field target shooters) will conduct individual tests at five-yard increments, or less, to learn exactly where the pellets are hitting at each distance.

The resultant information is recorded in the notebook for later reference, memorization, or transference to waterproof paper that can be taped to the gun.

Pellets. As stated earlier, the gun should be zeroed with the pellets that will be used most often in that particular gun. This is usually the pellet that produces the smallest groups with that gun. This may prove to be a flat-headed, match pellet at closer ranges, but a domed pellet at longer ranges. A hunter using an air pistol or lower-powered air rifle may choose a pointed pellet for its extra penetration, even if it's slightly less accurate than other designs in that particular gun. If the shooter is zeroing a new gun, some initial grouping tests should be done with an assortment of pellets to find the one style or brand that groups the best. In this case it is wise to buy a so-called "sampler pack" available through many airgun dealers. This is a package containing 20 or 30 pellets of several brands and styles and provides an economical way to find the best pellet for a particular gun.

Sight-Adjusting Tool. This will vary with type of sight. Many scopes are adjusted via coin slots under their turret caps. Aperture (peep) sights for target shooting may have knurled knobs that can be adjusted by hand. Sporting peep sights use flush-mounted screws that won't readily be knocked out of alignment under hunting conditions, but they do require a screwdriver for adjustments. Open sights may have stepped ramps for elevation adjustments and screws for windage adjustments. Some vintage airguns have sights rigidly mounted in dovetails that require drifting by hammer and punch (see *Adjusting Dovetailed Sights*, this section).

Spotting Scope: This optional accessory obviates a trip to the target to see where the pellets are grouping. When the scope is mounted on a tripod and pre-focused on the target, the shooter can stay positioned behind the gun and need only lean to the side to check progress downrange. Some airgunners equip their basement airgun ranges with small, inexpensive, closed-circuit TV cameras situated over the target, with the TV receiver back on the shooting table at the shooter's elbow.

Procedure

The following steps are generic and should apply to most airguns, irrespective of powerplant or sight system. Distinctions are made where necessary.

Ensure that the gun is unloaded and uncocked.

If sighting-in a spring gun, wait for any dieseling to "settle down." New spring guns may emit a sharp crack and whisp of smoke upon firing, caused by heat in the compression chamber detonating the lubricants in the cylinder. Such guns group erratically because of velocity fluctuations. Either shoot the gun until the dieseling stops, or clean out the lubricants and introduce new, high-flash-point oils. Many airgunners with suitable tools and skill will

routinely dismantle their new spring guns to hone the bearing surfaces in the power train and introduce new, non-dieseling lubricants.

Inspect the bore. If it's dirty, clean it (refer to maintenance section of each power system).

Tighten all stock screws.

Set up an appropriate shooting rest. Place required equipment on the rest (pellets, sight-adjustment tools, spotting scope, etc.).

Set up a paper target at typical shooting distance. Ensure that area beyond the target is safe. Set the target at the same height as the bore of the gun.

Load and cock gun, then get into shooting position using the improvised rest. As stated earlier, spring rifle shooters may get tighter groups when the forearm of the gun is rested on the palm rather than directly on the rest. CO_2 rifles and pistols are often placed directly on the rest. Firing a few shots in both modes should show which technique produces the best groups. Spring pistol shooters should hold the gun in two hands with only their wrists on the rest. The goal is to hold the gun motionlessly and without cant (i.e., without tilting it either left or right) during firing.

Take aim at the bullseye. Many open-sight shooters prefer to use a "6 o'clock" hold that does not obscure any part of the bullseye. When using this aim-point, the target circle appears to "sit" on top of the front sight like a golf ball on a tee. The sights will be adjusted upward, however, so that the pellets hit the center of the bullseye. Later, when hunting, the shooter will aim just under the squirrel's chin, with the pellet landing between the eyes. Shooters using scopes with thin crosshairs will generally aim at the center of the bullseye. Scope shooters may also want to "center" the windage and elevation adjustments and test for parallax error before sighting-in (refer to Scope Sights section).

Carefully and slowly squeeze off three to five shots using exactly the same grip and POA for each shot. The pellets will form a group somewhere on the target. If no hits show up, use a larger piece of paper.

Find the center of the group (the point halfway between its farthest edges) and determine how far vertically and horizontally it is from the bullseye. It may be, for example, one inch low and two inches to the right.

Move the rear sight in the same direction that the group should move to hit the center of the bullseye (i.e., to make POI meet POA). If the group was low and to the right, move the rear sight up and to the left.

Adjust elevation and windage sequentially, not simultaneously. Some shooters adjust elevation first, taking a shot after each incremental change to "walk" the POI to the right level, before moving on to the windage adjustment. If the sight is equipped with index lines (as are most scope and peep sights), the required number of clicks may be calculated as described in the previous section. For example, with a sight marked "one click = 1/4 inch @ 100 yds," 16 clicks will be required to move the POI 1 inch at 25 yds.

Trial-and-error adjustments will have to be made with sights that are unmarked, although a toothpick and a bit of white nail polish can create helpful, temporary indices.

Adjusting Dovetailed Rear Sights

As stated earlier, some rear sights are dovetailed in the receiver and will require "drifting" with a hammer and punch to make windage (left or right) changes. This requires a vise to hold the barrel, a small hammer, a brass punch, and two leather patches.

Procedure: After taking the initial shots to determine POI, clamp the barrel in the vise, protecting it from the jaws by cradling it in one of the leather pads. Next, note where the sight is positioned in the dovetail mounting. Use a toothpick and nail polish to paint a thin line across the sight and its mounting.

Next, place the second patch of leather against the base of the sight, position the punch against the base of the sight, and tap the sight lightly with the hammer in the direction you wish the POI to move. The sight will begin to move, as indicated by the separation in the paint line. Take the gun from the vise and shoot a couple of shots to gauge effect. Don't make gross changes. Usually, only a tiny movement is required to get the desired result out at the target.

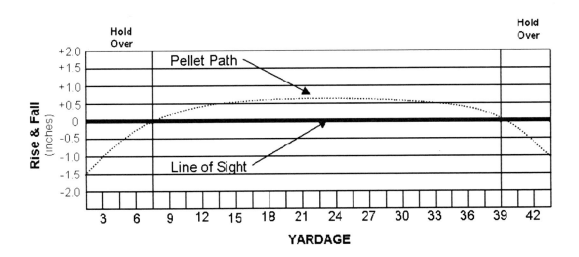

Figure 1. Pellet Flight Path. *Hypothetical path of a pellet fired from an ~800-fps .177 rifle with sights mounted one inch above the barrel. Because the muzzle is elevated during aiming, the pellet rises, then falls, intersecting the line of sight at two points in its travel: 7.5 yds and 40 yds (range at which gun was sighted-in). Unless fired from an elevated muzzle, a pellet begins to drop the moment it leaves the barrel. In example shown, shooter will aim slightly higher at targets less than 7.5 yards and more than 40 yards, and slightly under target situated between 7.5 and 40 yards. Heavier pellets traveling slowly will have a more curved ("rainbow") trajectory, requiring more compensation than this relatively flat-shooting pellet.*

Adjusting Dovetailed Front Sights

Some older airguns have dovetailed front sights. These can be tapped with hammer and punch to make windage adjustments. Follow the procedure described previously, with this exception: tap the sight to the left to move POI to the right; tap the sight to the right to move the POI to the left.

Zeroing with One Shot

This method requires an accurate, scope-sighted rifle (or pistol) and a rest that holds the weapon in a tight, vise-like grip, while still allowing it to be cocked and loaded.

Set up a blank sheet of paper at the desired distance, at the same level as the gun. Mount the gun in the holder and move it until the paper can be seen through the scope. Fire one pellet, then adjust crosshairs until they're aiming at the pellet hole.

Drifting a front sight with a punch.

Shooting at Ranges Other Than "Zero"

Figure 1 on the previous page shows the hypothetical trajectory of a pellet in relation to the gun's line of sight, as well as the areas where the shooter will "hold over" (aim high) or aim dead-on at targets appearing along the way. Although the precise amount of holdover or holdunder for each point may be calculated by using ballistics software (available on-line), it is more accurately determined by experimentation.

Set up paper bullseyes at 5-yard increments, with the distance marked on each sheet; aim dead on at each bullseye from a rest. Carefully fire a shot at each bullseye before leaving the bench. Gather up the targets and measure how far above or below the bullseye the pellets are hitting at each yardage. Record this information in your notebook, along with the brand, weight, and style of pellet used; changing any of those parameters produces another set of results.

Some hunters carry this information on laminated cards into the field or tape the card to the gun. They will then know, for example, to "hold over" 2 inches for that crow at 55 yards, but hold under 1 inch for a rabbit at 20 yds. Obviously, the shooter must also be able to judge distances accurately. This can be done with rangefinders, telescopes with variable power (explained in "Field Target Shooting" section), or by practicing in the field: estimating the distance to an object before pacing it off.

Shooting Targets High & Low

Pellets fired at a steep angle (i.e., greater than 45 degrees), up or down, will hit higher at the target than pellets fired horizontally at the same distance. A hunter shooting squirrels high in the oaks, or the ridge hunter after rabbits below him in an arroyo, must therefore aim lower than usual. Precisely how low is a matter of experimentation, although online calculators can give an estimate.

The procedure is simple. The squirrel or pigeon hunter should find a smooth-barked tree, select an elevated knot or blemish as an aiming point, then take a few shots from a stable position to determine precisely where the pellets are landing. The same type of informal experimentation should be undertaken for downward shots. Many shooters who know nothing about theoretical ballistics and trajectories have no difficulty with such shots, or even the amount of holdover or holdunder on level shots, because they've practiced with their guns extensively in a variety of situations.

AIRGUN SHOOTING

Plinking

Plinking, Defined

Plinking is informal shooting at inanimate targets. It gets its name from the sound a tin can makes when struck by a projectile. Plinking pointedly excludes bullseye target shooting (which is stupefying to a diehard plinker) and other types of shooting with defined rules and regulations, like field target and metallic silhouette. Although the exact origin of plinking is lost in the mists of time, it probably coincided with the introduction of the inexpensive, low-powered .22 rimfire and came of age when Daisy began mass-producing BB guns. Prior to that, shooting was a serious activity requiring effort and expense, and serious subsistence hunters or frontiersmen, many of whom were using muzzleloaders, were not likely to waste time and ammunition knocking cow chips off a fence post.

Plinking celebrates the fact that shooting, when not done for survival or Olympic fame, is loads of fun. There is really nothing more satisfying than standing *here* and knocking down something over *there*. All the better if that something breaks dramatically into a thousand pieces, or makes a resounding noise when hit. The key to high-quality plinking, then, is not only having the right weapon, but the right target. More on that later.

Plinking Airguns

Virtually any airgun can be used for plinking, but some are far more suitable than others. Remember, this is *fun* shooting and that means lots of shooting. A good plinking session can easily involve a hundred shots or more. Cocking and loading a single-shot spring gun over and over again, or pumping a pneumatic for each shot, will ruin the fun. The best plinkers are, therefore, effortless shooters, requiring little more than aiming and pulling the trigger. Obviously, CO_2 repeaters make ideal plinkers, especially if they're semi-automatics with high-capacity magazines. It's even better if they're bulk-filled, which allows more (and cheaper) shooting between recharges. Plinking tends to be a short-range proposition without the need for hair-splitting accuracy, so scopes and peep sights may be considered excessive. True, some shooters get into long-range can-busting and will demand a scope, but

Plinking is at its best with a fast-shooting, accurate repeater that uses cheap, plentiful ammo – especially when kids are doing the shooting. This vintage Hahn BB 30-shot repeater uses CO_2 – good for about 100 shots per gas cartridge. Reloading requires a quick flick of the wrist – no onerous pumping or cocking of a heavy spring. With its wooden stock, blued steel barrel, and exposed hammer, it has an old-west look that appeals to youngsters – the most important segment of the population to capture if the shooting sports are to continue in the US.

usually a good set of open sights will suffice for most plinking chores. Also, there are any number of inexpensive red dot and laser sights that can be affixed to the plinking rifle or pistol, and these are especially appreciated by kids. The laser sight projects a red spot of light onto the target, so the plinker can shoot from the hip with telling effect. Imagine squaring off against a row of soda cans on a fence with a semi-automatic pistol fitted with a laser sight. Imagine sending them flying, one by one, without raising the gun above the bellybutton. This not only makes the shooter look brilliant, but such shooting can become addictive.

For use with lead pellets only, this commercial target has paddles that swing up – and stay up – when hit. Hitting the center paddle releases them. Pellets flatten against the slanted backstop and collect in bottom of trap. This is a noisy target and its small size requires a peripheral backstop.

Plinking Targets

A good plinking target, by definition, will respond in some way to a hit. It must move, break, shatter, explode, ping, gong, or fall over, and if it does several of these things simultaneously, all the better. A hit must be obvious to the shooter and, more importantly, to any observers. A good plinking target will be cheap, readily available, and require little attention once the shooting begins. Ideally, the shooters can blaze away for extended periods without having to go downrange to service the targets. Most plinking targets will be objects orginally intended for other purposes, but there are several commercially available devices designed solely for this activity (illustrated). Some of these utilize falling paddles that can all be reset when the last paddle is hit. They have the added advantage of providing a backstop that traps pellets. Because of their extreme propensity for ricocheting, steel BBs should not be used when shooting at hard plinking targets, especially these mechanical devices. Lead BBs are acceptable, but are not necessarily interchangeable in guns that regularly shoot steel BBs.

Target Suggestions

The fevered brains of plinking junkies are continuously churning out new ideas for targets, and the list given here will be deemed rather pedestrian to them. It's a good starting place, however, and the objects listed below should provide many hours of shooting fun. Whatever is used, be sure to provide a safe backstop.

Cans: The venerable tin can has its fans. Try stringing them from trees at various distances, using stout cord. A full soda can, shaken, reacts spectacularly to a hit from a magnum airgun loaded with hollow points. The same goes for aersol shaving and cheese cans, which always seem to have residual gas. Suspended plastic bottles may also be used and they protest wonderfully when smacked by a flathead pellet. Cans with tabs can be strung like beads on a length of cord tied between two trees; they'll spin around the line crazily when hit on their hard base rims. Cans can also be set up as a pyramid and picked off one at a time.

Ice Cubes: A good, cheap, renewable plinking resource. Positioned along a fence rail, they shatter almost as nicely as glass without the attendant hassles. They may be made from colored water to add variety and improve visibility. If the cubes have time to melt before being hit, the shooter needs to work on speed and marksmanship.

Spent Firearm Shells: Empty cartridges comes in all sizes, are easily set up on their flat bases, and leap noisily when hit. Empty shotgun shells, particularly the brightly-colored plastic specimens, can take quite a beating from pellets and BBs and remain usable. Try slipping the empty shells over the tips of twigs at various heights and distances.

Toy Soldiers: The green or tan plastic soldiers can be bought by the bagful cheaply and they are virtually immortal unless hit by a magnum airgun. A few tanks

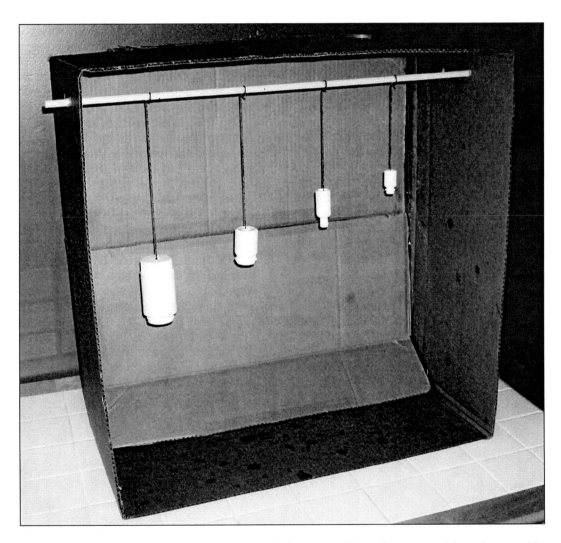

This target illustrates all elements of a good airgun plinking target. It's easily constructed from cheap, readily-available materials. The plastic bottles offer increasing degrees of challenge and they MOVE when hit (the sine-qua-non of a plinking target). The plastic surface limits ricochets and can absorb many dozens of shots before requiring (easy) replacement. The dowel across the top is wood, rather than metal, to inhibit ricochets. The cardboard panel in the back covers an old blanket folded to a thickness of three inches, sufficient for most low-powered BB and pellet guns. The target requires no re-setting, allowing the plinkers to stay safely behind the firing line for long shooting periods.

and planes are often in the bag, too. Shooters have been known to ascribe nationalities to the little guys, combining nationalism with plinking.

Balloons: Buy ballons by the huge bagful, fill them with water or air, and tie them to trees at varying distances. Although they have a limited life span, these are great introductory targets for little shooters. A more complex variant requires open space, a tank of helium, and a stopwatch. The filled balloons are released and shot out of the air after a pre-determined time period: the longer the time aloft, the harder the shot. This makes for very dramatic shooting, especially when multiple ballons are released, or the balloons are hit at high altitudes. Again, be sure that pellets will be landing in a safe area.

Edible Targets: Round candy wafers, which are multi-colored and sold in sheath wrappers, can be set up on their edges on a flat surface. They shatter satisfyingly when hit. Some shooters cut a long shallow groove in a length of 2x4 and use the trough to hold the wafers, or similar targets such as crackers. Other targets could include sugar cubes, gumballs, malted milk balls, etc. Cleanup is left to the birds and ants.

Homemade Spinning Target: This is easy to make, cheap, and re-usable. Flatten the bowls of a few old spoons with a hammer, then bend the handles into a loop and slip them onto a piece of hanger wire bent into a shape like this: П. A little more time with the pliers can create u-shaped indentations that will keep each spoon from sliding left or right. Shove the two legs into the ground and start shooting. When hit, the spoons will spin like propellers. Spoons of graduated size may be strung along the wire, providing an ever-increasing challenge from a single shooting distance. Avoid swiping any of those tiny, collectible spoons your aunt has hanging on a little wall-rack in the parlor.

Plinking and the Constitution

Plinking is the only correct, officially-approved way to introduce newcomers young or old to the shooting sports, especially airgunning. One does a true disservice to the shooting community when he tapes a bullseye to a box of newspapers and launches into a spiel about sight picture, controlled breathing, and trigger squeeze before forcing the newbie to make little holes in a piece of paper. Far better to set up some cans close enough so that a miss is unlikely and let the new person have at them. Newcomers to the hobby want to shoot and see things fall over, not listen to lectures on shooting theory. Once the tin cans start falling with regularity, have the shooter step back a few paces and try it again, and so on, until a real sense of accomplishment is achieved. This is the same principle used when taking a kid fishing for the first time. Hook a fish when the kid's not looking, then set the rod down. A minute later, casually ask the child to pick it up and "check the bait." New shooters have to experience that kind of *immediate fun* if their interest in shooting is to continue and they are to become defenders of the 2nd Amendment (of the US Constitution, that is).

Hunting Small Game

Introduction

The Law

Virtually every country in the civilized world has rules governing the use of its natural resources, and game animals are considered a natural resource wherever they're found. A nation's hunting rules define such things as permissible species, seasons, bag limits, and the equipment one can use in killing the animals. In the United States, numerous federal, state, and local laws all have their say in this activity, but it is usually one's state and local laws that have direct application. Hunting is typically the purview of a state's Department of Natural Resources or Fish and Wildlife Commission and they promulgate their rules and regulations in literature accompanying hunting licenses. However, local town or city ordinances may override these permissions and restrict the use of airguns, or even prohibit their ownership. Such local laws are not always promulgated widely. It behooves the airgunner to research the precise rules governing ownership and use of airguns by contacting the local district attorney, or by researching the laws at the City Hall or County Courthouse. Increasingly, state and local ordinances are available on websites. Obviously, one may also engage a lawyer who will, for a fee, conduct the necessary research and provide a precise determination of all the applicable laws. Airgunners are strongly advised *not* to seek information on local airgun laws from the local police department or the indigenous "cop on the beat." Usually the officer will issue an on-the-spot edict prohibiting *any* proposed activity involving an airgun, even if it eventually proves to be legal, and the pronouncement may be accompanied by confiscation of the gun. Once an accurate determination of the law is made, a copy of the ordinance *must* be kept available whenever and wherever the airgun is used.

Clean Kills

A "clean" kill is a quick kill that destroys little edible meat and causes the least amount of suffering. The cleanest kill is one that instantly halts the function of the animal's heart or brain, which are located in the quarry's "kill zones." With rabbits and squirrels, a pellet delivering approximately 3 foot pounds of energy (fpe) can provide a clean kill if the pellet is delivered to the brain or heart. An 8.6-grain pellet traveling 400 feet per second, for example, has the necessary energy. Many airguns can deliver that energy out to 50, 60, or 70 yards, but they may lack the accuracy required for a clean kill. The kill zones of a rabbit or squirrel are approximately 1 to 1.5 inches in diameter. Even if the gun is accurate enough to consistently group within those parameters at extended ranges, the hunter may not be up to the task. He or she may, however, be able to place all shots within a one-inch bullseye out to 25 yards. That will therefore be that individual's personal maximum effective range, which is a combination of the gun's power and accuracy and the shooter's skill level. That range may be extended with more practice, finer sights, better pellets, or by upgrading to a more accurate - not necessarily more powerful - airgun.

Shot Placement. Greater pellet energy will not compensate for poor shot placement. A squirrel gut-shot by a 130-fpe .22 long rifle firearm bullet may reach its den to die a protracted, painful death, whereas a hit in the brain by a 4-fpe airgun pellet would likely have killed the animal instantly. Again, it is a combination of pellet energy and shot placement that results in clean kills. Of the two, correct shot placement will result in more game in the bag than pellet energy, although neophytes tend to emphasize the latter. It may be surprising to newcomers to airgunning to learn that owners of match air guns generating little more than 6 or 7 fpe sometimes take them afield in search of small game. Although their weight and shape are awkward off the target range, their extreme precision can make them deadly in the right hands if ranges are kept within proper limits.

Pellet Energy

A responsible hunter should know the amount of energy his pellets are delivering to the target. Along with an honest assessment of his gun's accuracy and his

Pellet	Cal	Wt	Type	BC		Pellet	Cal	Wt	Type	BC
Beeman Silver Bear	.177	7.10	HP	.019		Marksman FTS	.177	8.8	R	.017
	.20	9.60	HP	.017			.20	11.1	R	.026
	.22	12.6	HP	.012			.22	15.0	R	.022
	.25	26.7	HP	.018		RWS Hobby	.177	6.9	F	.009
Silver Jet	.177	8.10	P	.020			.22	12.0	F	.010
	.20	10.7	P	.020		Supermag	.177	9.5	F	.012
	.22	15.2	P	.017		Meisterkugeln	.177	8.3	F	.011
Silver Sting	.177	8.40	P	.015			.22	13.9	F	.012
	.20	10.5	P	.016		Superpoint	.177	8.3	P	.011
Crow Magnum	.177	8.80	HP	.012			.22	14.5	P	.013
	.20	12.6	HP	.015		Super-H-Point	.177	7.4	HP	.010
	.22	18.6	HP	.014			.22	13.9	HP	.011
	.25	26.0	HP	.016		Superdome	.177	8.3	R	.014
Silver Arrow	.177	11.9	P	.016			.22	14.5	R	.013
	.20	16.0	P	.012		H&N Match	.177	8.2	F	.016
	.22	17.0	P	.017			.22	13.8	F	.011
	.25	24.6	P	.019		Sheridan Cylindrical	.20	15.1	R	.023
Kodiak	.177	10.6	R	.021		Bisley Superfield	.177	8.5	R	.019
	.20	13.3	R	.029			.20	11.5	R	.020
	.22	21.1	R	.031			.22	15.0	R	.016
	.25	30.7	R	.035			.25	24.6	R	.024
Laser	.177	6.50	R	.008		Crosman Premier	.177	7.9	R	.024
	.20	9.40	R	.012			.177	10.5	R	.032
	.22	13.0	R	.010			.20	14.3	R	.047
	.25	17.6	R	.008			.22	14.3	R	0.33
Perfect Rounds	.177	8.02	LS	.014						
	.25	23.6	LS	.020						

BC = Ballistic Coefficient   HP = Hollow Point   R = Roundhead   P = Pointed   F = Flathead

own marksmanship skill, he will use this information in deciding to take a shot or pass it up.

Calculating Energy. Pellet energy, measured in foot pounds (fpe), is a function of the weight and muzzle velocity (MV) of the pellet. The formula for calculating energy is:

FPE $= (MV^2 \times \text{pellet weight [grs]}) \div 450240$

Example:

MV = 625 fps; pellet wt = 8.6 grs
$625 \times 625 \times 8.6 \div 450240 = 7.46$ fpe

Pellet Velocities and Weights: Airgun manufacturers usually provide muzzle velocities without indicating the weight of the pellet used. A velocity figure without the pellet weight gives no indication of energy. A serious hunter will use a chronograph to measure the speed of the pellet, then use either the published weight for that pellet, or weigh the pellet himself, to calculate the energy that his pellet and rifle combination is generating. The table above provides the approximate weights of several popular pellets along with their head shape and ballistic coefficients (BCs; more on those later).

Airgunners without chronographs can research their weapon's (approximate) velocity in articles written by independent airgun writers or by querying the airgunners on online airgun forums. These sources, however, usually provide velocities and energies *at the muzzle*, not at the target. Unless delivering the *coup de grace*, hunters seldom shoot game at point blank range.

What hunters need are downrange ballistic data, i.e., velocity retention and energy figures *at the target*. A hunter could set up a chronograph at 30 or 40 yards and attempt to send a pellet over the machine's screens, thereby getting a true velocity reading at that range, but this is not always possible. Fortunately, a reasonably accurate velocity figure at various ranges can be calculated, as discussed in the section that follows.

Velocity and Energy Retention: In flight, pellets gradually lose speed and energy to influences such as gravity, wind resistance, and humidity. Some pellet designs retain velocity better than others because of their superior BC, which is a function of a pellet's weight, shape, and density. The table on the previous page provides BCs for a small sampling of popular pellets. If a shooter knows the muzzle velocity and the BC of the pellet he's using, he can approximate the remaining velocity of that pellet at any given range using this formula:

$$V@yds = MV \times EXP(-yds / (BC \times 8000))$$

For example, a pellet with a BC of 0.021 and an MV of 625 fps would be moving at 514 fps at 30 yards, as can be seen in the calculation provided:

$$V@Y = 625 \times (-30 \text{ yds} / (0.021 \times 8000))$$
$$V@Y = 625 \times (-30 / (168))$$
$$V@Y = 625 \times (-0.178)$$
$$V@Y = -111 \text{ or } 514 \text{ fps remaining at 30 yds}$$

In the above example, a pellet with a superior BC of 0.025 would have lost only 94 fps, versus 111, at 30 yds.

Once the shooter has determined the remaining velocity at a particular yardage, he can use that figure and the pellet's weight in calculating remaining fpe (see formula at *Calculating Energy*). In the previous example, a .177 pellet weighing 8.9 grains with a BC of 0.021 would have had a muzzle energy of 7.72 fpe. At 30 yards, that figure would have dropped to 5.22 fpe. A pellet with a BC of 0.025, starting at the same 625 fps, would have a slightly better remaining energy of 5.57 fpe.

Airgunners may purchase ballistics tables that provide approximations of pellet velocity, energy, and drop (i.e., trajectory, the rise and fall of the pellet in relation to line of sight) at all useful airgun ranges. These tables, which may also be found on the internet, use a pellet's starting velocity and BC in calculating downrange performance. Some websites offer programs that perform the calculations upon input of a pellet's MV and BC. However, these calculations sometimes differ from real-world results, so it is best to take one's gun out to the range and actually fire pellets at varying ranges to get a true picture of the performance of a particular gun/pellet combination.

Marksmanship, Importance of. Most of today's sporting air rifles deliver sufficient power to be deadly on small game out to 50 yards or more, as long as the hunter can place the pellets with sufficient accuracy.

Unless the hunter is using a gun of marginal power (as is the case with air pistols and match rifles), the critical factor in clean kills becomes marksmanship. The size of an animal's lethal zones varies by specie, but, as stated earlier, it is generally not much larger than one inch in diameter. It takes a good deal of skill to hit such a small target consistently at 40 or 50 yards, particularly when shooting offhand and in the excitement of a hunt. There is also the matter of anatomy: the hunter should know the location of the prey's lethal zones, and know them at the various angles at which the game may be encountered.

The sections that follow provide these locations for typical airgunning quarry, along with proven hunting methods for taking each species.

The Cottontail Rabbit

KILL ZONES: Brain shot is preferred, with neck and heart/lung shots a close second. Zones are approximately 3/4 inch for the brain, 1 inch for the neck, 1.5 inches for heart/lung shot. Both hunter and air weapon must be able to deliver a pellet to the kill zone with ~3 fpe for brain shots and ~4 fpe for heart/lung shots. Avoid hits elsewhere.

Habitat and Habits

The cottontail rabbit, like the squirrel, is a prolific, adaptable, and tasty little creature that thrives in almost every type of terrain. Suburban and agricultural sprawl has, ironically, made life better for the cottontail, at once providing new food sources and eliminating its traditional enemies - foxes, hawks, snakes, and human hunters. In many settled areas rabbits have become - like the white-tailed deer, the Canada goose, the black bear, and the cougar - a protected nuisance. Nevertheless, probably more cottontails are shot per-year than any other small game animal, and they are often the first true game species taken by new hunters. Virtually every bit of farmland, swamp, hill, or valley likely supports a population of cottontails, including city parks, backyard gardens, and municipal dumps. Like squirrels, cottontails don't hibernate; they're active all year 'round. They seek shelter and rear their young in underground burrows, brush piles, and briar patches, and it is in the vicinity of these places they are likely to be found. In fact, a farmer's field or a homeowner's lawn, if bordered by uncontrolled vegetation, is almost certain to harbor cottontails. Although they tend to be nocturnal, they can usually be found feeding along the edges of fields in the early morning and late afternoon.

Hunting Techniques

The traditional firearm method for taking cottontails is to roust them out in the company of another hunter or short-legged dog and nail them with a shotgun or semi-auto .22 when they explode from cover. This approach won't work for the airgunner with a short-range, single-shot weapon. He can't send a load of shot after a fleeing bunny, and the spray-n-pray approach, even if he's using a semi-auto airgun, likely won't result in a clean kill. The airgunner seeking rabbits is advised to wait until he has a motionless rabbit within range of his weapon. This may seem an unlikely scenario given the cottontail's speed and nervous temperament, but it can be arranged in any of several ways. These are explained in the sections that follow.

Walking Them Up: In this method, the hunter walks very slowly through known rabbit territory and either looks for a rabbit or waits for one to burst from cover. Rabbits are clever at concealment, however, and, unless there is snow on the ground, they will be difficult to discern from the surrounding vegetation. They usually aren't seen until rousted, and hunters are often startled by rabbits bursting from a patch of brush or tangled grass previously deemed "empty." If that hunter had been walking quietly and slowly (one soft step every ten seconds or so), the fleeing rabbit probably wouldn't have gone too far, possibly remaining within range. The hunter should calmly take aim as the rabbit is running and hold fire until the critter stops. Should the rabbit stop before the gun is raised, the hunter is advised to wait several moments for the animal to "settle in" before *very slowly* bringing the gun fully to shoulder and taking aim. Here's a tip: for some unknown reason, a fleeing rabbit will often stop in its tracks if the hunter whistles sharply.

Tracking: This method, a variation of walking-them-up, requires the hunter to be abroad early in the morning after a fresh snowfall. This can be the most magical time to hunt, especially if the sun is shining in a cold, blue sky. Rabbit tracks will be visible and recent, and following them to a brush pile or clump of dried grass and weeds can be very productive. It is often possible to discern the eye or ear of a hunkered cottontail under these circumstances. Tracking in the snow almost invariably gives the hunter a better idea of where the rabbits are than tramping about on uncovered ground. Also, the sparkling snow and the clarity and contrast it brings to the formerly drab rabbit patch make for a more enjoyable hunt. There are some rabbit hunters who will venture out *only* after a nighttime snowfall, perhaps more interested in the setting than the shooting.

Stalking: This method requires a visible specimen and an avenue of approach, such as when rabbits are out feeding in low vegetation. This is not traditional stalking, where the quarry remains oblivious of approaching danger until the last moment, a feat perhaps achievable only by blacksnakes, cats, and determined little boys with BB guns. Rather, the rabbit stalker will likely be after a specific animal that is fully aware of his presence. The trick here is to give the bunny a false sense of security, to make it feel that the tall human sidling toward it intends no harm. This means that the hunter will take small, nearly-silent steps, and then only when the rabbit drops its head to feed or is otherwise distracted. The stalker would do well to have his gun at the ready, to avoid looking directly at the rabbit, to spend much time motionless, and to assume, in general, a non-threatening demeanor. Although this is not the most effective method of rabbit hunting, many hunters will find that they can indeed get within range by such stalking. Should the rabbit hop off into cover, the hunter may choose to sit down, settle his gun into position, and await the animal's return. This will often happen within minutes if it's feeding time and the animal was only slightly alarmed.

Lamping: This method is legal and popular in various countries in Europe, where farms and estates are often overrun with rabbits. In this method, a stealthy hunter carries a powerful electric lamp into the rabbit fields, switching it on every now and then to see what lies ahead. The light not only illuminates the scene, but momentarily bewilders the quarry, allowing a shot to be taken. Typically, the lamp is mounted atop the scope or on the hunter's head, and the 6-volt battery is slung around the shooter's waist. Red or orange filters are used instead of white light, which is more likely to frighten the animals. The switch for the lamp is usually activated by the hand supporting the rifle. Lampers frequently familiarize themselves with their shooting areas in the daytime, looking not only for game, but potentially dangerous spots in the landscape. British hunters have enhanced the effectiveness of this already deadly method by using silencers on their airguns. Rabbits oftentimes feed in close proximity to one another, and a silenced weapon can achieve multiple kills before the remaining rabbits in the group catch on and head for cover.

The Gray Squirrel

KILL ZONES: Brain shot is preferred, with neck and heart/lung shots a close second. Head presents smallest kill zone but is generally best. The squirrel is legendary for taking hits in other areas and living long enough to crawl to safety. Both hunter and air weapon must be able to deliver a pellet to the kill zone with ~3 fpe for brain and neck shots and ~4 fpe for heart/lung shot. Avoid hits elsewhere.

Habitat and Habits

The gray tree squirrel is a time-honored, toothsome airgunner's quarry. These prolific, resourceful, and not unattractive little creatures have resisted the encroachments of man and may be found wherever there's food, shelter, and water. Since they eat nuts and berries and live in hollow tree trunks or high, leafy nests, the best place to find them will be in mature hardwood forests laced by creeks or streams. Hunters should scout likely areas in the pre-season (usually early September) for tell-tale "cuttings" on the forest floor. These are the remains of hickory nuts, acorns, or walnuts dropped by feeding squirrels. Like many forest creatures, squirrels are most active around dawn and dusk, although they will extend their hours during fall days when the nut harvest is at its peak. Squirrels do not hibernate, but they loathe leaving their warm, stocked nests on those wintry days that give pause even to an avid hunter. They may emerge, however, on clear, still days to seek water or to sun themselves on a high limb in the weak sunshine.

Hunting Techniques

Walking Them Up: In this type of squirrel hunting the airgunner, who will be carrying string and pebbles in his pockets, moves slowly and quietly through a likely area, watching for movement in the treetops and,

more importantly, listening for squirrel sounds and activity. The walking will be very quiet and very slow, a single, soft footfall every few seconds. The goal is to get within shooting range of the critter without startling him into a hightailed race to his den.

Squirrels are noisy creatures, and this helps the hunter who is walking them up. Not only do they bark and chatter when communicating with each other or when scolding intruders, but their travel and games of tag produce scratching sounds on tree bark and loud swishes as they spring from one bough to another. They are noisy on the ground, too, often making quite a racket as they scratch in the dry leaves for misplaced nuts. They are noisy even when sitting on a limb eviscerating an acorn. Their gnawing can be heard for some distance in a quiet wood, as can the steady rain of nut cuttings trickling down through dry autumn leaves to the forest floor. Hunters will use these sounds not only to pinpoint the location of their quarry, but to cover the sound of their own approach. Once a squirrel is spotted, a stalk can begin. A soft footfall, heel first, is necessary to get within shooting range. Also, keeping another tree between hunter and the squirrel will hide the approach. It's very difficult for a hunter to approach a squirrel he can see – because the squirrel can see the stalker. A hunter who can get within airgun range of a squirrel without alerting it is an admirable woodsman. Usually the animal spots the hunter and makes a dash for its den. Some, however, will bark loudly and rapidly, tails flashing, scolding the intruder and alerting the rest of the squirrel population. Others will simply move around to the far side of the tree and wait.

The airgunner can do little about the fleeing squirrel, but he has a good chance with the barker and the hider. The barker's curiosity will often keep him in view long enough for the hunter to get off a shot, and there are ways to get the hider out into view. The hider circles the top of the tree while the hunter circles the bottom. This continues until the hunter remembers the pebbles and string in his pocket. A few pebbles tossed to the far side of the tree may trick the squirrel into coming around to the hunter's side, and if they don't, the string can be tied to a bush and paid out as the hunter moves to the other side of the tree. When the squirrel moves to the far side, the hunter takes aim in the general area of the squirrel, then tugs on the string. The moving bush will often scare the squirrel into moving back again — right into the hunter's sights.

Still Hunting: Still hunting for squirrels involves placing oneself in the midst of known squirrel habitat in a comfortable, seated position, gun at the ready, and waiting until a squirrel comes into shooting range. While waiting, the still hunter moves only his eyes and head, and moves them slowly. Once a candidate is spotted, the hunter raises the gun inch-by-inch, to avoid startling the prey. In this type of hunting, the shooter often will have time for precise aiming and a controlled trigger squeeze.

Diligent still hunters will generally take up position early in the morning before the squirrels are abroad, although this is not absolutely necessary for success. Squirrels will soon resume normal activities once a late arriving hunter has sat down and become a motionless part of the forest. In some cases, the animal's natural inquisitiveness will actually cause it to approach the hunter. Most still hunters will wait for several animals to congregate and begin feeding before taking the first shot. The low report of an airgun often won't scare the remaining animals back to their dens. Frequently they will simply pause to watch their stricken companion fall to the forest floor and then resume feeding. If the hunter stays put, marking the location of his first victim for later retrieval, he may often take a second or third animal from the same location. Every movement, of course, is made with exaggerated slowness, even when lowering the gun after taking a shot. A missed shot under these circumstances may sometimes only startle the intended target, who may not know what caused the noise. Here the hunter will refrain from reloading and taking aim, remaining motionless until the animal has settled down and resumed its activities.

Camouflage: Although many jurisdictions require the wearing of blaze orange during hunting, there are places and circum-stances where camo can be worn safely and legally by a squirrel hunter. A squirrel hunter wearing the right camo and sitting motionless in the forest will very likely have the advantage over another hunter sitting nearby in everyday garb. Some may argue that squirrels are hardly as discerning as turkeys or deer, that camo is more of an affectation than an advantage. That may be true of the blotchy military camo worn by paramilitary types, but not of the civilian camo available to serious hunters. Commercial camo recreates in stunning detail virtually every type of background a hunter is likely to encounter. It's available as articles of clothing, coverings for one's weapon and gear, and as enclosures for one or more hunters. Perhaps the deadliest camo of all, and the most expensive, is the so-called 3-D, textured suit that obliterates even the tell-tale human outline remaining with regular camo and transforms a man into a patch of background vegetation, shivering leaves and all.

Blinds: For hunters who can't sit still, or who would like to be able to move around unseen to take shots in any direction, there are lightweight, portable tents fitted with shooting slits. As with camo clothing, these are available in numerous patterns to suit the terrain and season. They set up in minutes, hide the shooter from his prey, and afford a degree of warmth and element protection denied the shooter sitting out in the open. For the hunter wanting a simpler and more economical blind, there are bolts of camo netting that can be strung on rods in the ground surrounding the hunter. Although these provide no roof, per se, they can be arranged to provide a degree of overhead cover. The least expensive blind, of course, is the enclosure fashioned from onsite vegetation. Here the hunter sinks a couple of Y-shaped sticks in the ground, stretches another pole across them, and then leans boughs, brush, and branches against the horizontal pole to form the "hide," as it is sometimes called. Obviously, small gaps are left in strategic places for seeing and shooting. Shooters often equip their blinds with seating of some type and experienced hunters learn to evict any resident insects prior to settling in. When possible, natural blinds should be set up a few days before the shooting session to accustom the squirrels to its presence.

Calls. Hunters who bother to learn squirrel calling swear by it; those who haven't tried it believe it gimmicky. It is so effective because squirrels are variously inquisitive, helpful, or territorial, and these traits are exploited rather easily by a good call and caller. The best way to learn calling is to buy a kit that includes the call - a pocket-sized, bellows-powered device - and a video of an experienced caller in action. After a bit of practice, the hunter will soon be able to tap on the bellows, or shake the call like a rattle, and produce the sounds that arouse anger, curiosity, or compassion.

The so-called squirrel whistles are perhaps the deadliest calls of all; they imitate the terrified squeals of an infant squirrel caught by a hawk or fox, bringing the local squirrel population out in force. The experienced hunter using such a whistle will accompany the squeals with the violent rustling of leaves on the forest floor, which imitates the throes of predator and victim caught in their life and death struggle. Squirrel calling can be very effective if done properly, and it's particularly advantageous to the airgun hunter armed with a short-range weapon.

Hunting Vermin

The Rat

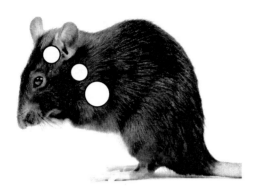

KILL ZONES: Brain shot is preferred, with neck and heart/lung shots a close second. Zones are approximately 0.5 inch for the brain and neck, 1 inch for a heart/lung shot. Both hunter and air weapon must be able to deliver a pellet to the kill zone with ~2 fpe for brain shots and ~3 fpe for heart/lung shots. Avoid hits elsewhere.

Rats are classified as *vermin*, which affects their status as an airgunner's quarry. Vermin, in the purest sense, are un-protected pest species that may be killed during any season of the year, on any day of the week, at any time of day or night, and in any quantity. That definition may be restricted by local laws here and there, but vermin, whether furred or feathered are typically unsympathetic creatures, with few advocates in high places. Often they are an introduced specie that competes with indigenous populations for food and space. Usually small and prolific, vermin have become the treasured quarry of airgunners the world over, and although these shooters may lament, for example, the vast numbers of rats, starlings, and pigeons that befoul the planet, they would surely hate to see their efforts result in complete elimination. This section considers the lowly rat and offers strategies for pursuing it with an airgun.

The first Norway rat is believed to have arrived in North America as a stowaway aboard a sailing vessel, disembarking via mooring lines when the ship docked. Although some hold that domesticated rats make intelligent and affectionate pets (and even tasty meals in some cultures of the world), the wild Norway rat is voracious, destructive, prolific, cunning, often disease-ridden, and – when found in a dump or slum – cursed with an appearance generally inspiring revulsion. It is not surprising then, that it is a prime target of the airgunner, whose accurate, low-powered, and quiet weapon is ideally suited for this type of hunting. Many farmers beset by rats are hesitant to use traps, poisons, and firearms that could harm their livestock or buildings. They are often receptive, however, to the skilled airgun rathunter who can offer a degree of vermin control with negligible collateral damage should a pellet go astray.

Rats live wherever humans live, often in intimacy, with the two species separated by mere inches of masonry or sheetrock. They abound wherever there is food, cover, and inept predators. The greatest concentrations, therefore, are found in cities rather than suburbs or farmland, especially those areas of a city where garbage is allowed to accumulate. Unless diligent measures are taken to discourage them, rats will invade any structures they find desirable, especially food processing or storage facilities, restaurants, and grocery stores. Often they will live in security in the infrastructure of luxury apartment buildings and travel by night through tunnels, sewers, and alleys to food sources in less tidy areas of the neigh-borhood. Rats thrive even where garbage is collected regularly, emerging nightly to forage in dumpsters behind restaurants and supermarkets before the morning pickup.

Out in the farmlands, virtually every livestock barn will have a population of rats, no matter how many cats, snakes, or owls are deployed against them. Docks and other waterfront areas are often heavily infested, especially if the areas are associated with fish processing, sewage release, or located near seaside res-taurants, boardwalks, or amusement parks. The occasional rat may be glimpsed in broad daylight in any of its habitats, but it is under the cover of darkness that the marauding hordes emerge. The successful rat hunter, therefore, will become as much a creature of the night as his quarry.

Rat hunting requires both specialized equipment and a degree of dedication (or dementia) not possessed by the average airgunner. This is partly true because of the diversity of rat habitats, each requiring unique adaptations in method or equipment. Hunting rats in a chicken coop, for example, requires equipment and techniques different than those used by an apartment dweller shooting back-alley rats from his bedroom window (yes, this occurs), or by the rathunter cruising garbage pickup areas behind the local strip mall at 2 AM (yes, this, too).

Equipment

Guns: A rat must drop in its tracks when hit. It must not be able to escape to die (and decompose fragrantly) behind the woodwork. For that reason, many rathunters choose .22 caliber over .177, not only for greater knockdown energy, but to avoid the overpenetration of a high-speed .177. All things being equal, the .22 pellet will realize greater energy than the .177. That means greater shock to put the rat down and keep it down, especially if the hunter concentrates, as he or she should, on head shots. Any rifle or pistol with sufficient precision and power to deliver ~4 fpe to the chest of a rat – or ~3 fpe to its brain - can be used for ratting, providing the shooter has the skill to hit a kill zone barely larger than a nickel.

Pellet Style: Many rathunters choose flat-headed match pellets because they deliver more shock than penetration. Hunters using domed pellets will sometimes cut an X on the nose of each pellet with a razor, then smooth it over before loading it into the gun. This causes the head of the pellet to peel back on impact, limiting penetration and creating a more destructive wound. Hollow-point pellets will expand similarly, but only if launched with sufficiently high velocity. The rathunter is advised to experiment with various types of pellets by shooting into bars of clear glycerin soap positioned at the distances he expects to shoot. Each pellet's penetration, expansion, and "wound channel" can be assessed fairly accurately in this manner.

Sighting and Lighting Systems: For daytime ratting, any sighting system should suffice, although a low-powered scope (2X) with a big, light-gathering tube will generally have the advantage over iron or peep sights. Such a scope not only allows rapid target acquisition, but gives increased visibility to an animal known to lurk in the shadows. Rats are most active after dark, however, so the hunter must either bring light to the scene or multiply ambient light. Some hunters strap small flashlights to their guns or scopes and flick them on periodically, usually when they hear scratching or squeaking. Others affix spotlights to their gun or a headband. These are powered by 6-volt batteries strapped to the shooter's waist and controlled by pressure switches mounted near the trigger. Since this white light can frighten rats, most hunters cover the lens with a less-threatening red filter and use it with a scope with an illuminated reticle. Some hunters use the red light in conjunction with a laser sight. Using no lights at all is least threatening to rats, and they can indeed be shot in darkness by hunters using night vision scopes. These sophisticated devices gather and multiply ambient light within the scope, allowing the shooter to observe, and settle the crosshairs upon, completely unsuspecting rodents.

Strategies

Bait Stations: Rats travel along established routes within their neighborhoods, but, when they're out in the open, they rarely sit still long enough for the airgunner to take careful aim. The efficient rathunter will pre-determine his quarry's route, then smear peanut butter in an advantageous place along that route. The rat will not be able to carry away the delicacy, as they are wont to do, and the hunter will be able to get off a shot when the animal pauses for a lick. Some hunters will even place an impromptu backstop behind the bait station to catch any stray pellets.

Motion Sensing Lights: Some shooters will equip the hunting area with motion sensors that turn on a red-filtered light each time a rat appears. If the hunting area is near the shooter's residence, the sensor can be wired to the house to alert him via blinking light, buzzer, or computer message that there are rats at the feeding station. Such a light setup is often allowed to operate for a few nights to acclimate the animals to its eerie, red glow.

Ultraviolet light: Another type of light coming into use is the ultraviolet light used with theft detection powder. The powder is placed in an area where the rat is certain to brush against it, transferring it to its fur.

When the animal passes beneath a pre-positioned ultraviolet lamp, the powder glows, allowing the hunter to see it in the darkness. He can then take aim with a scope equipped with an illuminated reticle.

The Starling

KILL ZONES: A starling about to raid a songbird's nest. Overlay indicates kill zones and their relative sizes, but the starling's small size ensures that hits virtually anywhere will bring the creature to the ground. A brain shot is preferred, with neck and heart/lung shots a close second. Zones are approximately 0.5 inch for the brain and neck, 1 inch for a heart/lung shot. Both hunter and air weapon must be able to deliver a pellet to the kill zone with ~2 fpe to drop the bird.

Like the Norway rat, the starling is an introduced specie. It was brought to New York City from England in the 1890s. As the story goes, a deeply misguided fan of William Shakespeare transported app-roximately 50 birds to our shores so that America might have all the birds mentioned in the bard's plays. An omnivorous and aggressive creature slightly smaller than a robin, the starling is now one of the most common birds in North America and, along with the pigeon and Canada goose, one of the most detested.

Description

The starling's black or brownish plumage sports an oil-slick greenish/purple iri-descence. The creatures temporarily develop white tips on their feathers after molting, giving them a speckled ap-pearance. Their beaks are yellow in spring but turn brown in winter. Short tail feathers give these birds a triangular silhouette in flight.

The starling's "song" consists of either a contented warble with a clicking subtext, or an occasional rising and falling whistle. Starlings eat anything organic, nest in every type of natural or man-made structure (often driving other bird species from their nests, then eating the eggs or young), and roost in numbers that can reach the millions. In certain areas, they are held in the same regard as rats. It is not surprising then, that airgunners probably shoot more starlings each year than they do any other living creature, rats included. Along with the English Sparrow, they are usually the first "game" the young nimrod brings down. In fact, many adult airgunners continue to pursue starlings long after they've hung up their Red Ryders, citing the service they are doing to humanity and indigenous bird populations. Unvoiced is the truth: the thrill they feel at hearing the *thwock* of a pellet knocking a starling off a distant barn roof, or seeing that puff of feathers and that somersaulting descent to the ground. Starling shooting is so popular, in fact, that there are entire websites devoted solely to this activity.

Equipment

Guns: Starlings do not have the thick, protective plumage of crows and pigeons and are not particularly difficult to kill, however, this does not mean that low-powered airguns should be used against them. They will move to more distant perches at the sight of an armed human, so an airgun with good reach and accuracy is required. Some shooters prefer high-speed (i.e., >700 fps) .177s over the .22, citing the flatter trajectory of the smaller caliber, but a .22, properly sighted in, will be at no disadvantage. All things being equal, the heavier pellet will retain more of its initial velocity than the .177, deliver more energy upon impact, and be more wind-resistant. Keep in mind that domed pellets are usually more accurate at extended ranges (i.e., beyond 50 yds.) than flatheads or pointed pellets.

Starlings are cautious and will flee when they detect movement, especially a human trying to cock an airgun. With that in mind, some shooters prefer a gas ram over a spring gun, since the gas-rammed gun can remain cocked for long periods without fear of spring damage. Perhaps the best choice of weapon is a repeating PCP rifle, set to low velocity to avoid overpenetration, because it be cocked and fired with minimal commotion. Unless the birds are close-in, as in the garden-shooting scenario described below, the shooter is well-advised to use a scope. A starling is little more than a black dot at 50 yards, and peeps, red dots, and open sights may be too coarse for drawing a bead on such a small target. In jurisdictions that allow it, a silencer provides an immeasurable advantage, as any urban hunter will attest.

Strategies

Backyard Safaris: Shooting greedy, quarrelsome starlings off the birdfeeder, from which they've evicted all other "decent" bird species, is a popular but secretive activity in many suburban neighborhoods. It usually starts with the exasperated homeowner borrowing a BB gun and shooting from a window or back door - out of view and earshot of the neighbors - and ends with the purchase of a more suitable eradicator. The ranges involved are typically short, so a low-powered airgun with open sights is acceptable, provided it is accurate and quiet. Obviously, the shooter must determine where his pellets will go after missing - or completely penetrating - a bird. Many a feeder has been damaged by an over-anxious (i.e., unsafe) shooter. Some shooters will position a wooden backstop beyond the feeder or will extend the landing bar on the feeder to a safer distance. As stated, this type of shooting is often done from within the house, ensuring that the sight and sound of the weapon will be undetected. Shooters after bigger starling "game bags" typically graduate to the techniques described below.

Bait Stations and Blinds: A starling bait station is nothing more than a feeder designed to deliberately attract living targets. In consideration of the starling's wariness, the station should be set up in the open away from cover where predators may lurk and it should be at least 6 feet above the ground. It can be as simple as a flat board affixed to the top of a pole. A favorite bait is common suet, which should be placed in a wire suet basket sold by wild-bird feeding supply stores. Do not use the hanging chain supplied with many of these feeders as it will sway when a bird lands. Obviously, the station will attract all birds, but starlings will usually chase them off. This activity requires patience. Like crows, starlings prefer to land in a reconnaissance area before proceeding to the feeder, so this should be considered when siting the station. The "blind" may be the shooter's home, or a garage or shed with a window overlooking the station. Out in the woods, a blind may be a commercial camouflage tent, camouflage netting strung across rods, or a structure fashioned from natural materials. The blind should hide the cocking and loading movements of the shooter, yet provide ports for aiming.

The Crow

KILL ZONES: Brain shot is preferred, with neck and heart/lung shots a close second. Zones are approximately 0.5 inch for the brain and neck, 1 inch for a heart/lung shot. Both hunter and air weapon must be able to deliver a pellet to the kill zone with ~3 fpe for brain shots and ~4 fpe for heart/lung shots. However, side shots through the folded wing into the chest cavity require more energy and pointed pellets.

Few sounds are more distinctly rural than the cawing of crows on a foggy dawn, and even those farmers who despise the creature would miss that sound if it were ever permanently silenced. Although this large, intelligent bird can be a depredatory nuisance, and there are even some bird lovers who decry its nest-raiding tendencies, one should not assume that they can be shot on sight. Crows are classified as vermin in many areas, but it is wise to check with the local Department of Natural Resources before venturing afield after them.

Habitat and Habits: Virtually all areas of the northern hemisphere support crow populations, although, like all creatures, they are most abundant where there is much food and few predators. More will be found, therefore, in settled farming communities than in pristine forests. Omnivorous and opportunistic, the typical crow may have corn-on-the-stalk for breakfast, dumpster french fries for lunch, and flattened roadside rabbit for dinner. Crows are active throughout the day, but tend to take it easy in the heat of summer afternoons. Although solitary at times, crows will nonetheless congregate to share a good meal, mourn a fallen comrade, watch a fight between two other crows, and, of course, to lynch an owl caught in the open in daylight.

In that last circumstance, a great throng can be assembled in mere minutes to satisfy the crow's weird bloodthirst for the beleaguered owl. Their innate curiosity and gregariousness play a part in this, for no crow will pass up a gathering of his cohorts. The cumulative din from the excited assemblage can be deafening. While watching the fights or tormenting an owl, crows will abandon their vaunted caution, even when a shooter is near. This carelessness, however, does not apply to foraging crows. Foragers will post a sentinel who will sound the alarm at the approach of danger, and these animals are quite discerning. They learn at an early age to flee a human carrying a weapon, but will allow golfers and fishermen to approach within yards. Other crow idiosyncrasies include a fondness for collecting *bling* – shiny bits of glass, metal, sunglasses, keys, etc. - and storing it away in knotholes, although hunters have yet to find a way to exploit this tendency.

Equipment

Guns: Although a light sporter air rifle generating 12 fpe can take crows to 30 yards, such power should be considered the minimum for this type of hunting. Unless hit in the head or neck, a crow can be a tough bird to kill. It is well-armored in feathers that can be surprisingly difficult to penetrate. Even a direct chest shot won't drop the bird if the pellet hits the tough breast bone. For this reason, many veteran airgunning crow hunters will choose a magnum springer or PCP in the 20-fpe range in .22 caliber and load it with pointed pellets. A repeater will have the advantage in those situations where the birds are coming thick and fast. Sighting equipment for this rapid-fire, short-range type of shooting tends toward open sights, low-powered scopes, red dots, and wide-windowed holographic sights. High magnification scopes with their limited field of view can be a liability in most crow-shooting scenarios, which are described in the sections that follow.

Strategies

Decoys, Calls, and Blinds: As stated earlier, crows are curious birds and will invariably flock wherever their brethren are gathering. They follow their ears initially, then swoop in once they spot the source of the clatter. The airgunner will capitalize on this by setting up a blind in a likely area, putting out some crow decoys (or, better yet, an owl decoy, as discussed in the next section) in a visible area, and then sending out invitations with either a lung-powered or electronic crow call. Pre-hunt scouting will help to find a productive area, which could be a patch of woods at the edge of a cornfield, a clearing in a forest, or an overgrown brush pile bordering a dump. It's a good idea, if possible, to set up the blind a week or so before you hunt to acclimate the crows to its presence. The blind may be constructed of natural vegetation and fitted with "windows" in the walls and roof, or it may be a commercial camouflage tent blind that can be set up in minutes. The latter are available in patterns to match the season and local flora and are fitted with floors, windows, doors, and ventilation openings. The blind should be positioned near the decoys, but it should also be within range of a crow "landing zone," particularly if the decoys are set out to mimic birds feeding on the ground. Crows like to land on some nearby elevated structure for a little reconnaissance before dropping down to the ground. The hunter will, of course, have his weapon trained at that landing zone and know precisely where his pellets are hitting at that range[9]. The decoys may be cut from cardboard using a picture as a pattern, then spray-painted black and fitted with glued popsicle-stick legs. Commercial decoys are more realistic and have eye hooks so they can be fitted with string and hoisted into the trees. The battery-powered call with amplified speakers, though less-portable than lung-powered calls, can be devastatingly effective in luring crows. CDs are available that play such hits as *Crow Reveille*, *Crow Death Cry*, *Crow Distress*, and *Crow and Hawk Fight*. The airgunner need only set up his blind, position the decoys, turn on the call, and sit back and wait. Once the crows start landing - and falling - the action can become chaotic, especially if the hunter adds one more item to the mix - the owl decoy described below.

Owl Decoys: As stated, crows have a visceral hatred for owls and will harass any they happen upon. Their screaming invective draws other crows until the hapless creature is surrounded by a dive-bombing mob. Crows in such a frenzy will often ignore the fact that some of these "owls" never move a feather (or even have feathers), and that many of the others crows are falling dead to the ground, inexplicably, one by one. An owl decoy positioned atop a pole in a clearing, along with the broadcast screams of other crows, will invariably draw a crowd to an airgunner's blind. There are reports of dozens of crows being taken in this way, and many an airgunner crouching in a blind with a spring gun has wished for a multi-shot PCP or CO_2 gun in such a situation.

Miscellaneous Attractants: Dead crows will draw live crows, who are either cannibalistic or maudlin, so it is helpful during a shooting session to leave the deceased scattered about until the living wise up and finally depart. Another productive ploy is to place a dead rabbit or other critter, entrails enticingly exposed, in the middle of a farm road or open area, and set up a blind nearby. Again, it is advisable to place the corpse near an elevated landing zone and to put a few decoys around it. A CD of some screaming crows or a few blasts on a call should produce action. The hunter should allow a few crows to arrive and get comfortable before taking a shot at the next candidate to swoop into the "recon" area. Another dependable crow attractant is a black plastic garbage bag stuffed with trash from a fast-food restaurant. Placed strategically near the hunter's blind and the "recon" area, its contents spilling about, a garbage bag is a sure-fire crow lure, especially when accompanied by decoys and a screaming crow CD.

Eating Crow: Along with pigeons (*squab*, to gourmets) crows are one of the few species of vermin that is not only edible, but

---

[9] The airgunner should do some pre-hunt shooting at elevated targets to determine where the pellets are grouping when fired at various angles. A crow-sized silhouette will give a good idea of the marksmanship required under actual field conditions.

quite palatable. Most recipes for dove and quail can be adapted for those who fancy roasting the entire plucked bird, but many crow hunters prefer to use the breast meat only – in the form of two walnut-sized chunks of meat – and discard everything else. The breast meat is removed by slicing the bird's belly left-to-right just under the ribs, slipping a couple of fingers into the slit and – taking hold of the feet with the other hand - pulling skin and feet in opposite directions. This lays bare the breast, allowing the two chunks to be sliced away from either side of the breastbone. There are recipes that involve stews and shish-kebobs, but, at camp, many hunters will simply roll the breasts in flour and fry them in shortening.

TARGET SHOOTING

Field Target

Typical field target match showing squads of shooters at their lanes; scorers; spotters; a match director; and spectators separated from the contestants by a rope. Photo (c) P. Mateus, Portugal.

Field target shooting, a relatively recent invention of British origin, is a competitive activity in which the participants use airguns to knock down targets that simulate typical airgunning quarry: crows, rabbits, squirrels, rats, etc. The targets are usually placed in a natural setting over a marked course, although matches are sometimes held at open fields that provide the required distance and safe backgrounds. Open to air rifle or pistol shooters, most of the emphasis is placed on air rifle competitions.

The metal targets, set at ranges from 10 to 55 yards, fall flat when hit in their "kill zones," but remain upright when struck anywhere else. The circular kill zones vary in diameter. Fallen targets are reset by a string extending back to the firing line. The targets may be placed on the ground or fastened to trees, stumps, or rocks, forcing the shooter to assume a variety of stances. Under the governance of a match director, shooters follow formalized rules relative to equipment, scoring, time-per-shot, etc. The rules provided in this section are based on those promulgated by the American Airgun Field Target Association, although groups do hold matches according to their own homegrown rules. It is this informality and camaraderie that accounts, in part, for field target's popularity. Distance esti-

mation, often down to a yard, is critical to this game, however, at this writing, rules do not permit rangefinding equipment separate from the gun.

Field target shooting is an appealingly uncomplicated activity. The targets are set up at various distances within delineated lanes, usually two or three targets to a lane, with perhaps 10 lanes for a match. The targets in the lane are fired upon in a specified sequence (nearest to farthest, for example), and the shooter may not step outside the lane when taking a shot. Contestants group themselves into squads of two or three: on rotation, one contestant shoots while the others keep score, monitor timing, and reset fallen targets. Each match will have a Director to resolve disputes, assisted by marshals.

Divisions/Airguns/Caliber

Classes are segregated by the type of airgun, ensuring that the competitors are evenly matched at the outset. Some clubs establish power limits to preclude target damage (the sport started in England with guns limited by law to 12 fpe). At this writing there are three divisions:

1. PCP – any pre-charged pneumatic airgun may be used, with any type of sight.

159

Field Target rifles have evolved into highly specialized machines. This Air Arms EV2 PCP is designed specifically for field target and costs approximately $2K USD. Uses compressed air from SCUBA tank. Extreme precision and adjustability are hallmarks of a winning rifle. The large focus adjustment wheel serves the same purpose as the adjustable objective bell housing on other scopes, but can be operated without removing the gun from the shoulder; yardage markers are printed on the wheel. 826 fps with 7.4-gr pellet for 50 shots (100 shots per fill). Approx. 42 inches; 9 lbs.

2. Piston – any spring piston airgun may be used, with any type of sight.

3. Hunter – any sporter airgun using any type of power (CO_2, spring, PCP, pump pneumatic), with scope sights limited to 12X or less.

So, there's room for just about any shooter in the field target game, but only specialized guns will be competitive when the shooting gets really organized and serious. An inexpensive CO_2 or pump pneumatic won't cut it, especially when going up against guns that can easily group three shots into a 1/2 inch circle at 50 yds. Even super-accurate Olympic match guns won't work because they don't have the energy to trip the paddles at extended ranges or buck the wind on gusty days. No, a good field target gun is a specialized device, an airgun, ironically, no hunter would likely take afield. They're certainly capable of taking live game, but the sighting equipment and ancillary doo-dads (scope wheels, stock-adjusting appendages, etc.) make them unsuitable for hunting. Most shooters choose .177 caliber over larger calibers for its flatter

trajectory and because the "skinnier" .177 can slip into the kill zone and hit the paddle where a .20 or .22 might hang up on the "lip."

Targets

The mechanized target is the signature feature of this activity, and it's evolved considerably from its beginnings in late 20th century England. In those days, shooters pasted paper bullseyes on wooden or metal cutouts shaped like rats, rabbits, or other typical airgunning quarry, and then shot at them with the guns they used when hunting their flesh and blood counterparts.

Eventually, some shooters devised hinged, re-settable targets that fell flat when hit. This was more satisfying than paper-punching, but provided little challenge for a good marksman with an accurate airgun and even "wounded" animals were likely to fall over.

In time, the shooters developed targets that would drop only when hit in the specific "kill zone." As stated, the kill zone

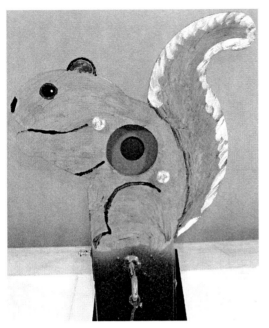

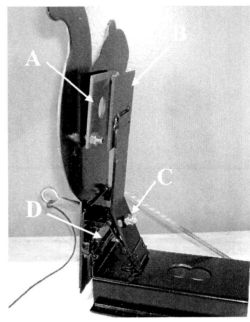

Photo at left shows front of typical field target. Made of heavy steel and crudely hand-painted, the target will likely be repainted many times throughout its lifetime. Hole in "kill zone" is a bolted metal plate that can be replaced with one of smaller diameter to increase challenge. The target will not fall unless pellet flies through hole and hits paddle. The kill zone hole, seen from rear of target, is shown at A in photo at right, with paddle (B) directly behind it. The paddle is hinged to allow it to fall and pull down the front plate, which is also hinged (D). Paddle sensitivity can be adjusted by screw (C). Cord attached to eyebolt extends back to firing line so target face can be pulled upright to reset. Base of target is staked into ground or strapped to tree limb.

is a small hole in the target, roughly corresponding to the kill zone on a living animal, behind which is a metal paddle and sear. If a pellet gets through that hole - and the holes vary in size from 0.5 to 1.5 inches - the paddle will trip a sear that allows the target to fall flat. Targets are designed so that pellet fragments or split pellets usually will not activate the mechanism. Field targets are produced in geometric shapes for those who can't abide the shooting of even inanimate "animals."

At this writing, field target manufacturing is principally a cottage industry practiced by a handful of hobbyists in the US and England, although some major airgun companies are beginning to manufacture and sell their own targets. Virtually all of the hobby craftsmen advertise and distribute their wares via the internet. Prices are around $40US per target, which is inexpensive considering the handwork involved.

Some manufacturers produce target faces of wood, others work strictly with heavy steel. The wooden-faced targets have a radius of protective steel surrounding the kill zone. Animals represented by these targets are too numerous to mention. Some of them are whimsical, like the frog-on-a-toadstool target produced by one manufacturer. Others are custom-created by manufacturers who build to suit

Rangefinding using a scope: the shooter aims at the target, focuses the image by adjusting the ring on the objective bell, and then reads yardage printed on the bell housing. Some scopes use a sidewheel for focusing rather than the adjustable objective at front of scope.

One reason for field target's popularity: the picturesque settings that can often be arranged when locale permits. Field target shooting offers participants and spectators a level of visual and auditory satisfaction that paper-punching competitions can't equal.

if the customer provides a picture or sketch of the desired "animal."

Positions

Any position is allowed, unless a lane specifically designates kneeling or standing. No supports other than the shooter's arms or body are allowed. Some targets may be placed to force the shooter into a specific position. A padded seat or "bum bag" may be used if it's no higher than 6 inches.

Timing

To keep a match moving along, the Match Director may restrict shooters to one minute per shot, using a timer, beginning when the gun is brought to the shooter's shoulder. Failure to fire before the timer sounds is counted as a miss.

Rangefinding

Pellets descend steadily and predictably during flight. A pellet that just makes it over the rim of the kill zone at 42 yards will

likely have dropped just enough to nick the rim of the hole at 43 yards, resulting in a miss. It's relatively easy for a shooter to know how far the pellet will rise above or drop below the line of sight at any given range, and then aim accordingly, but it's not as easy to determine the range. No airgunner can eyeball 30 or 40 different stretches of ground during a match and correctly estimate the distance to the target often enough to be competitive. Separate rangefinding devices are not permitted, but there is a solution: certain scopes have rangefinding capability. Read on.

The Scope as Rangefinder

A scope of 18X or more can be used as a rangefinder provided it has an adjustable objective lens (i.e., a focusing front lens) with a yardage index on the bezel. Using such a scope, the shooter need only aim at the target, twist the front ring until the image comes sharply into focus, then read the yardage indicated on the bezel. Higher magnification allows sharper focusing for more accurate distance estimation, with 18X being about the minimum necessary to get the required resolution. Some shooters use scopes of 30 or 40X. However, field of view decreases as magnification increases, and this can make target acquisition difficult. For this reason, many shooters use scopes with variable power (ex. 8-40). The lower magnifications can be used to find the target, the higher magnifications for distance estimation.

Pellet Drop Compensation

A field target shooter must raise the muzzle of the gun to compensate for pellet drop, ensuring that the pellet will keep its head up long enough to drop down into the kill zone. If the target is 45 yards away and the pellet will drop, say, 1 inch below point of aim at that range, the shooter may either aim an inch higher on the target (guessing at what constitutes an inch), or adjust the elevation of the crosshairs so that she can aim directly at the kill zone. Some field target shooters use a third option - a scope equipped with a reticle that has several hold-over/hold-under reference points, each providing a specific, pre-determined amount of compensation.

Adjustable objective showing yardage markers and dot reference, indicating target at ~41 yds. Field target shooters will not rely on such wide, imprecise markers, but will focus on targets set at measured yardages, then mark the scope accordingly in smaller, more precise increments.

By far, most field target shooters adjust the windage and elevation knobs for each shot, allowing them to place the crosshairs directly over the kill zone. As discussed earlier in the section on scope sights, each "click" of adjustment will change the point of impact a specific amount. In our example, it may require, say, eight "up" clicks to raise the point of impact that required one inch at 45 yards. Obviously, this is information that the shooter has determined (and annotated in a handy notebook) prior to the match.

Metallic Silhouette

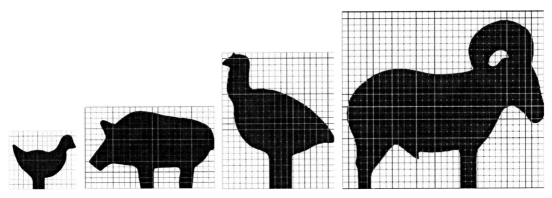

Relative sizes of steel silhouette targets: chicken, pig, turkey, and ram. The National Rifle Association and the International Handgun Metallic Silhouette Association (IHMSA) specify dimensions and distances. The ratios are maintained as sizes decrease for lower-powered weapons and shorter ranges. Targets are set at varying distances, chickens closest, rams farthest. The targets are welded to steel base pedestals, whose dimensions are similarly prescribed. For high-powered firearm rifle events, the rams are 27 inches high, 32 inches long, and set at 450 yds. Rams for air rifle events are one-tenth size: 3 ¼ inches long, 2 ½ inches high, and are set at 45 yds.

Background

Metallic Silhouette derives from a Mexican shooting contest (*siluetas metalicas*) in which live chickens, turkeys, pigs, and rams were tethered to stakes at 200, 300, 360, and 450 yards, respectively, and fired upon with long-range rifles. Shooters using big-game or, more often, cheap, military-surplus weapons took turns at the targets, shooting offhand only, often while fellow contestants passed the tequila and kept up a barrage of good-natured, deliberately distracting, taunts. Far off at the targets, scorers safely ensconced in bunkers emerged to check the animals after each string of shots. Drawing a single drop of blood counted as a hit, prompting some shooters to aim low

and send wounding sprays of dirt and gravel at the animals. Attempts were made to export this activity north into the United States, but it never caught on, even among devotees of pigeon and turkey shoots that used live birds. Many American shooters did, however, travel to Mexico to participate.

Eventually, life-sized steel silhouettes replaced the animals. Positioned at the original distances, these heavy metal targets had to be knocked completely over for the shooter to score a hit. Now - less gruesome, and offering a good degree of auditory and visual gratification for both spectators and participants - the sport crossed the Rio Grande and took root in the States. Targets soon were reduced in size and range to accommodate rimfire and

Table 1. NRA Air Gun Silhouette Classes

	Target Air Rifle	Sporter Air Rifle	Open Air Rifle	Iron Sight Pistol	Any Sight Pistol
Gun	Any unaltered factory target spring, pneumatic, or CO_2 gun.	Any unaltered spring, pneumatic, or CO_2-powered rifle weighing less than 11 lbs, including scope. Up to .22. No ball or non-lead ammo.	Any spring, pneumatic, or CO_2 gun weighing less than 16 lbs. Up to .22. No ball or non-lead ammo.	Any spring, pneumatic, or CO_2 pistol. Up to .22. No ball or non-lead ammo	Any spring, pneumatic, or CO_2 pistol using any type of sight. No ball or non-lead ammo
Sights	Any	Any	Any	No optics or electric; no hooded sights	Any
Restrictions	No additional slings, butt hooks, palm rests, gloves, or shooting jackets. No round or non-lead ammo.	No additional slings, butt hooks, palm rests, gloves, or shooting jackets. No round or non-lead ammo.	No additional slings, butt hooks, palm rests, gloves, or shooting jackets. No round or non-lead ammo.	No optical or electric sights. No additional slings, butt hooks, palm rests, gloves, or shooting jackets	No additional slings, butt hooks, palm rests, gloves, or shooting jackets

pistol shooters. This "shrinking" principle was inevitably carried a step further to bring the challenge and fun of silhouette shooting to airgunners.

The activity is now sanctioned by the NRA and the International Handgun Metallic Silhouette Association (IHMSA), with both groups promulgating rules (see Tables 1 and 2) and organizing matches.

"freestyle" events. Shooting freestyle, the competitor may stand, kneel, sit, or lie down, however, no artificial support (i.e., the ground, shoe sole, or boot top) may be used to stabilize the gun.

Matches can be 40, 60, or 80 rounds. In a 40-rounder, competitors shoot at 10 chickens, 10 pigs, 10 turkeys, and 10 rams. In a 60-rounder, they shoot at 15 of each

Table 2. IHMSA Air Pistol Silhouette Classes

	Production Open Sight	Production Any Sight	Unlimited	Unlimited Any Sight	Unlimited Standing
Cost	$150 max.	$150 max.	No cost limit.	No cost limit	No cost limit
Barrel	10.75 in. max.	10.75 in. max.	15 in. max.	15 in. max.	15 in. max.
Weight	4 lbs. maximum	5 lbs. max.	5 lbs. max.	6 lbs. max.	6 lbs. max.
Sights	No optics, no tube sights; no covered rear sights	Any sight unmodified from original.	No scopes or other optics.	Any. Max. length 18 inches	Any sight unmodified from original
Position	Freestyle	Standing	Freestyle	Freestyle	Standing

In **air rifle silhouette**, targets one-tenth the size of the originals are fired upon at distances one-tenth as far:

- chickens at 20 yards
- pigs at 30 yards
- turkeys at 36 yards
- rams at 45 yards

In **air pistol silhouette**, the same targets are used, but at even shorter distances:

- chickens at 10 yards
- pigs at 12.5 yards
- turkeys at 15 yards
- rams at 18 yards

Although the animals differ dimensionally, the distances at which they are placed make them each appear the same size to the shooter.

Tables 1 and 2 provide the various classes and equipment for NRA and IHMSA airgun silhouette classes (these are general guidelines current as of this writing; the organizations both maintain websites and provide current rules). Note that NRA matches are fired in the standing position only, whereas IHMSA matches include

type of critter, and 20 of each in an 80-round match. Competitors shoot at the animals in banks of five of each type, with 2.5 minutes allowed for each bank.

Silhouette contestants are ranked by skill level, but compete side-by-side. Determining an individual competitor's skill level is explained in the section that follows. Unlike Olympic shooting competition, silhouette does not provide a less rigorous course for females.

Skill Classifications

Silhouette competitors are ranked by skill level, allowing beginning and intermediate shooters to win in their class even when competing against seasoned experts. Beginners shoot their first match in the "unclassified" category, and that first score determines their ranking in the next match (i.e., Master/International, AAA, AA, A, and B). Tables 3 and 4 provide the equivalent scoring ranges for NRA and IHMSA skill classifications based on a 40-shot match. A competitor moves to the next highest class when she achieves two scores on that level within 12 months. If she fires a score that is 2 or more classes above the current class, she

Table 3. NRA Skill Classifications

Target Rifle		Sporter Rifle		Open Rifle		Open Sight Pistol		Any Sight Pistol	
Master	32-40	Master	29-40	Master	34-40	Master	30-40	Master	36-40
AAA	26-31	AAA	23-28	AAA	28-33	AAA	23-29	AAA	30-35
AA	20-25	AA	17-22	AA	21-27	AA	16-22	AA	22-29
A	13-19	A	11-16	A	15-20	A	8-15	A	15-21
B	0-12	B	0-10	B	0-14	B	0-7	B	0-14

Table 4. IHMSA Skill Classifications

Production Freestyle		Production Standing		Unlimited Freestyle		Unlimited Standing		Unlimited Any Sights	
Int'l	38-40	Int'l	28-40	Int'l	40	Int'l	36-40	Int'l	40
AAA	33-37	AAA	22-27	AAA	37-39	AAA	30-35	AAA	37-39
AA	24-32	AA	16-21	AA	30-36	AA	22-29	AA	0-36
A	18-23	A	8-15	A	25-29	A	15-21		
B	11-17	B	0-7	B	18-24	B	0-14		
C	0-10			C	0-17				

advances to the class immediately below the class of the score fired, effective at that match. For example, an A shooter firing an AAA score, will advance to the AA class. Shooters may be in 2 or 3 categories simultaneously if shooting in 2 or 3 equipment classes (ex., Master in Target Rifle and AAA in Sporter Rifle).

Score Conversion

Scores from 60- or 80-round matches may be converted to an equivalent 40-round score for determining skill classification. 60-round match scores are converted by multiplying the score by 2, dividing the result by 3 and dropping any fraction of a point. 80-round match scores are converted by dividing the score by 2 and dropping any fraction of a point.

Shooting a Silhouette Match

The match director explains the rules before the match, calls Start and Stop times, and arbitrates disputes. Targets are presented in banks of 5 (five chickens, five pigs, etc.) and must be fired upon in a left-to-right sequence. Shooters have 2.5 minutes to down each set of 5 targets. A typical match presents 40 targets, requiring the shooter to fire two series of shots at each animal (or 3 series of shots for a 60-shot match).

Targets are shot consecutively from left to right. One shot is fired at each animal. If the shooter misses one target, he moves on to the next animal. Any animal shot out of sequence is considered a miss. Scoring is simple: if the shot knocks the target completely over, it's scored as a hit. Anything else is a miss. Moving the target doesn't count. Targets not fired upon in the 2.5-minute time limit are scored as misses. After the shooting period, the scores are recorded and the targets reset.

Metallic pig silhouettes set up for a 60-round match. Targets are on a metallic rack. Targets must fall over, not merely move, for the shot to count. Shooter is allowed 2 ½ minutes for each set of 5 targets.

Olympic Target Shooting

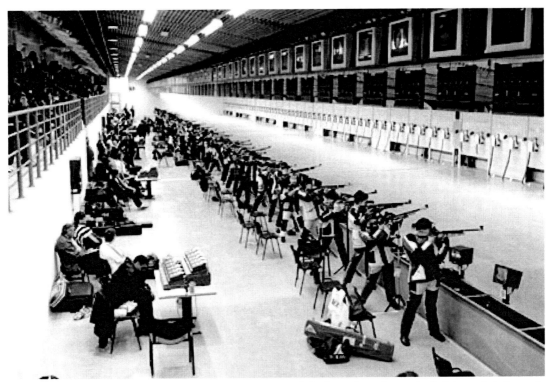

Olympic-style air rifle venue showing spectator's gallery (left), line of coaches and officials, and phalanx of contestants, each firing at an electrically-scored target that projects shot results instantly on large, overhead screens at upper right and on smaller screens at each shooter's station. Spectator interest has increased dramatically with introduction of these visual scoring features. Instantaneous tallying allows spectators to know immediately who's winning and who's coming up from behind. Bank of printers in foreground provides hard-copy record for post-mortems. Photo (c) P. Mateus, Portugal

Air rifle competition became an Olympic event in 1984. Air pistol shooting did not become an Olympic event until 1988. At this writing there are events for men and women in air rifles and pistols, and, at times, one Running Target event. Certain events are co-ed, while others are segregated and provide a less-demanding program for women. The Running Target event is for men only. For all three events, shooters fire at black bullseye targets with 10 concentric scoring rings.

Currently, USA Shooting is the governing body for the Olympic shooting sports in the United States. Headquartered at the Olympic Training Center in Colorado Springs, Colorado, USA Shooting trains and selects the teams that represent the United States at World Cups, World Shooting Championships, the Pan American Games, and the Olympics. It also manages development programs and sanctions events at the local, state, regional, and national levels.

Once a year, USA Shooting hosts the National Junior Olympic Shooting Championships. At this event, competitors who have shot a qualifying score in their State's Junior Olympic matches vie for places on the national development team and the opportunity to compete at the national and international level. Several months before the Olympic Games, the members of this elite shooting group compete for slots on the U.S. Olympic shooting team.

Basement targeteers with Olympic ambitions should contact USA Shooting for information on the local matches that could ultimately lead to a gold medal. For rifle, pistol, and running target events, shooters fire at round, black aiming areas displayed on white backgrounds. The targets are divided into 10 concentric scoring zones with graduated point values, as a typical bullseye target. However, at the Olympic level, the targets are scored via an acoustic system that precisely locates pellet holes

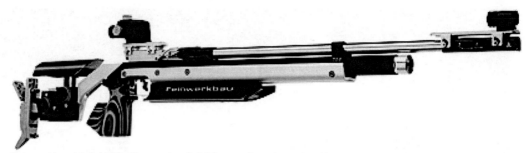

Feinwerkbau Model 700 Olympic-level, PCP air rifle. Adj stock, sights, trigger; ~600 fps; 43 inches; ~10 lbs.

within a few hundredths of a millimeter. These targets look the same as paper targets at 30 feet, but do not have scoring rings. Computers instantly score each shot and televise the scores on large monitors for the spectators. The competitors also have small monitors at their shooting stations that instantly display the position of the last shot, the current total score, the number of shots fired, and the location of previous shots.

Specialized shooting clothes (jackets, gloves, and shoes) that help to restrict body movement are allowed for the rifle and running target events, although there are rules governing their use. Air pistol events, however, do not allow the use of such clothing.

Air Rifle Events

In the air rifle events, competitors stand and shoot lead pellets from .177 caliber guns at targets 33 feet away. The bullseye, or 10-ring, is 0.02 inch in diameter.

Guns: The guns may be air- or gas-powered and weigh up to 12 pounds. No optical sights are permitted. Trigger weight may not be less than 17.6 ounces. There are also restrictions on barrel length and stock dimensions.

Course of Fire: Men take 60 shots in one hour and 45 minutes, while women have one hour and 15 minutes for 40 shots.

Perfect Match Score: For men, 600 is perfect and 592 is world-class. For women, 400 is perfect and 394 is world-class. In the air rifle competition, the central "ring" must be completely shot out to register a score of 10 when using such targets.

Finals: The top eight competitors advance to a 10-shot final round, with 75 seconds allowed per shot. The final is calculated in tenths of a point and added to the match score to determine winners. A perfect final score is 109.

Perfect Aggregate (Match + Final) Score: 709 for men, 509 for women.

Air Pistol Events

In the air pistol events, competitors stand and shoot lead pellets from .177 caliber guns at targets 33 feet away. The bullseye, or 10 ring, is 0.45 inch in diameter.

Guns: Any .177-caliber (4.5 mm) pistol powered by air or gas may be used in this event. Weight may not exceed 3.3 pounds. The overall size of the pistol is limited to a length of 16½ inches, a height of 7.9 inches and a width of 2 inches. No part of the grip or accessories may enclose the hand. Only open and metallic sights are allowed.

Course of Fire: Men take 60 shots in one hour and 45 minutes, while women have one hour and 15 minutes for 40 shots.

Perfect Match Score: For men, 600 is perfect and 585 is world-class. For women, 400 is perfect and 385 is world-class.

Finals: The top eight competitors advance to a 10-shot final round, with 75 seconds allotted for each shot. The final is scored in tenths of a point and added to the match score to determine medalists. A perfect final score is 109.

Perfect Aggregate (Match + Final) Score: 709 for men, 509 for women.

Running Target

In this event, which is not always scheduled at Olympic venues, the shooter stands and fires at the target from a distance of 33 feet (10 meters) while it is pulled along a track measuring 6 feet, 7 inches (2 meters). The shooter may not shoulder the rifle until the target appears. The target moves at fast and slow speeds, covering the span in 5 seconds for slow events, and 2.5 seconds for the fast event. There is also a segment in which the speeds are mixed in an order unknown to the shooter. The event was originally designed to be a bloodless replication of the snap shooting practiced by hunters using targets that were silhouettes of deer or boar. Now the target consists of two bullseyes placed six inches apart, with an aiming dot between them to assist the shooter in tracking. The 10-ring on each bullseye is 0.20 inch (5 mm) in diameter.

Guns: Any .177-caliber (4.5 mm) rifle powered by air or gas weighing 12 lbs (5.5 kilograms) or less may be used in this event. Telescopic sights of 4X or less are permitted. Most major target air rifle

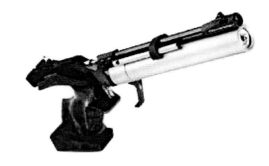

Feinwerkbau P44 Olympic level pre-charged pneumatic pistol. .177 caliber; 16 in; ~2 lb; adj. trigger, sight, grips; 450-500 fps.

manufacturers build guns specifically for use in Running Target events.

Course of Fire: Shooters fire a total of 60 shots, 30 on the fast run, 30 on the slow run, and 40 on the fast (to consist of 20 slow and 20 fast in a sequence unknown to the shooter. On the slow run, the target is exposed for 5 seconds. On the fast run, 2.5 seconds.

Perfect Match Score: 600 is perfect, 575 is world-class.

SELECTING AN AIRGUN

This section provides a review of the various factors that must be considered when selecting an airgun, including . . . .

THE AUTHOR'S FIRST TIME: LESSONS LEARNED

THE PERILS OF THE SPORTING GOODS STORE

A NOTE ABOUT AIRGUN POWER

PURCHASING CONSIDERATIONS:
    A. PURPOSE:
        i.   Hunting Small Game:
            Caliber
            CO_2 in Hunting Use
            Single-Stroke Pneumatics
            Ergonomics
            Excess Power
        ii. Hunting Large Game
        iii. Plinking
        iv. Training
        v. Target Shooting
    B. COST
    C. MAINTENANCE
    D. THE HASSLE FACTOR

AIRGUN REPAIR FACILITIES

The Author's First Time: Lessons Learned

Not everyone buys that first airgun in their formative years, but this writer did, in the early 1960s at the age of twelve. I'll relate a bit of the story here, because it points up issues to be considered when buying an airgun, whether one is twelve or fifty.

At the time, I really didn't want an airgun, *per se*. An airgun was a fall-back position. I wanted a Stevens Model 15 single-shot .22 rimfire rifle. Exactly why I wanted the Stevens had something to do with gunwriters touting the virtues of learning to shoot with single-shot weapons (i.e., safety; making the first shot count, etc), as well as the fact that the Stevens had a clean, purposeful look, an interesting cocking knob protruding from the back of the bolt, and it cost a mere $15. Nevertheless, there would be no firearm in my life at that time. Although I had unfettered access to 500 acres of woods and fields teeming with small game just over the fence behind my house, it was situated in a suburb just 30 miles from New York City, where my father was a cop. I was awash in anti-gun sentiment, even before assassinations became the national pastime of the '60s.

Finally, after much pleading (and memorizing the 10 Commandments of Gun Safety), my father agreed to let me get an air rifle, but I would have to pay for the gun and ammunition myself. Well, an airgun was still better than my homemade slingshot and blowgun, so I got a paper route ($6 a week) and scoured my Gun Digests and other available sources of airgun information (quite meager in those days).

I learned there were several airguns sufficiently powerful for hunting small game, which would be the gun's primary use. Although there were some American offerings, the really interesting airguns seemed to come from Europe. Apparently, the Europeans had resorted to airguns because they had plenty of firearm laws and little open space, whereas Americans had plenty of space and few gun laws. There was the Webley Mark III springer at $80, some Crosman and Benjamin pump and CO_2 rifles at around $30, and the Sheridan Blue and Silver Streaks for $27.50. I eliminated CO_2 guns due to the extra expense for gas cartridges (plus, I had swallowed the then-current marketing nonsense about "troublesome seals" on CO_2 guns). The cost of the Webley and the other European spring guns seemed exorbitant, and I really wasn't convinced that a single cocking of a spring could deliver the necessary punch. What finally convinced me was a photograph in a Sheridan pneumatic rifle advertisement . . .

The picture showed a cutaway of a block of wood penetrated to ever-increasing depths by pellets launched from the Sheridan rifle. To a kid of 12, who had previously believed an air rifle was a mere BB flinger that might dent a soup can, this was a revelation. Here was a gun that was acceptable to the timid anti-gun "authorities" surrounding me, yet was capable of delivering animal-killing power. Needless to say, I hid that photo from my parents and started saving up.

After what seemed like years, I had the money for the gun and a can of pellets ($2.50 for 500). I soon learned that my deliberations had led to a perfect choice. The purchase of that Sheridan led to countless magical days afield. Not a single acquisition before or since (yes, even a motorcycle) has provided so much satisfaction. I can photographically recall patches of woods and meadow that yielded up squirrels and rabbits and, on one stunning occasion, a Canada goose (it took hours to pluck). Even today, the scent of oil like the one used by Sheridan on their pellets can transport me back to those long-ago days.

What does this reminiscence have to do with the intelligent selection of an airgun? It illustrates the basic issues that must be addressed before laying down money for an airgun: Purpose; Cost; Maintenance; and Hassle Factor.

Each of these is discussed in the sections that follow. It is wise to have a firm grip on them before heading to the internet or the local sporting goods store. Before we discuss them, a few words should be said about sporting goods stores (and gun shows) that sell airguns.

The Perils Of The Sporting Goods Store

Why should one be wary of the local sporting goods store when purchasing an airgun? Because the person behind the counter often believes that merely taking position in front of a long rack of rifles, shotguns, and airguns magically confers upon him knowledge that you – a mere customer – do not possess. When it comes to guns, rare indeed is the [male] shopkeeper or counter clerk who will admit even the slightest smidgen of ignorance on the subject. Any question you pose about airguns will likely be answered with an absurdity, delivered with certainty and assurance. Thus, your inquiry about the relative power of pump guns and springers, for example, will elicit something like this:

"Let me tell you something, this here spring gun Beeman makes will give you a helluva lot more power than any pump gun. Ha! This baby gets over 1000 feet per second with one cock while that there Sheridan might hit 600 if you pump it 15 or 20 times. Don't kid yourself, this Beeman's right up there with a 22 long rifle." Then, as if to underscore all the erroneous, misleading statements he just uttered[1], he might even cock the spring gun and fire it, without a pellet, at the ceiling just to let you *hear* the power in that loud crack (which is actually the sound of the piston head fracturing itself on the far end of the compression chamber).

Even in those rare instances when the individual behind the counter *does* know airguns, he may try to get you to buy something he feels is more appropriate to your needs (which will always be more expensive than your choice). A salesman of this stripe will use the common trick of offering his explanation in front of an assemblage of other customers, forcing you to be publicly stalwart and contradictory, something he has already sensed is not in your nature. No, the best way to buy an airgun at a sporting goods store is to stride into the establishment confidently and ask for the specific gun you have previously researched and selected, accepting no substitutes, displaying the same sureness of purpose you would have when ordering a sandwich at a deli counter. The only way to get that certainty is to develop an answer for each of our four major purchasing issues: Purpose, Cost, Maintenance, Hassle Factor: Before that, however, it may be wise to consider how airgun *power* is communicated to the buying public, because it is this one issue that generates the most interest and misinformation.

---

[1] Beeman does not make airguns; the company distributes airguns made by others. A 16-gr Sheridan pellet traveling at 600 fps will carry more energy than a 6-gr pellet travelling at 1000 fps. The most powerful spring guns generate about 35 foot pounds of energy, whereas a .22 long rifle firearm generates ~140 foot pounds. Finally, 8 is the factory-recommended maximum number of pumps for a Sheridan rifle; the air from extra pumps either stays in the gun when it's fired, or causes airlock.

A Note About Airgun Power

Airgun power is measured in *foot pounds of energy* (fpe). As stated in the introduction to the chapter on hunting, the advertised muzzle velocity of an airgun's projectile does little to convey the power of the gun. One must know the fpe generated by a particular airgun in order to assess its suitability for a particular species of game animal. Manufacturers advertise the velocity of their guns, knowing that high muzzle velocities will seduce the ignorant. They usually will not, however, provide that one essential piece of information that is needed to calculate the true power generated by the gun – the *weight of the pellet used* in achieving those blistering speeds.

As a sophisticated airgunner, the reader must assume that manufacturers or distributors used the lightest available pellet in their velocity tests. In .177, that would be about 6 grains; in .22, approximately 12 grains.

Using the formula for fpe (muzzle velocity squared X weight of pellet (in grains) / 450240) we see that the aforementioned shopkeeper's 1000-fps spring gun develops 13 fpe with a 6-grain pellet, while the Sheridan he insolently dismissed develops 14 fpe with its 16-grain pellet, a pellet, by the way, that is manufactured of an alloy that ensures maximum penetration.

The fpe figures cited throughout this section should be used as a general guide. Although animals have been killed with seemingly miniscule fpe, it is always better to hit an animal (in that vital area, of course) with more energy than less. This will prompt some to ask, "Well then, why not just use a firearm if you're all that concerned?" Anyone reading this book should be able to cite half a dozen reasons why firearms, under certain circumstances, are simply out of the question.

Purchasing Considerations

PURPOSE

People buy airguns for any of a host of reasons, sometimes requiring that the gun do double or triple duty. However, it is usually best to determine a principal use for the prospective gun, and then get one that fits the bill. The subsections that follow present a few of the more common applications for airguns and the attributes of weapons appropriate for the category.

Hunting Small Game

The general rule is to match the gun and projectile to the animal you intend to hunt, being certain that it has the power and accuracy for a humane kill. So how much power is enough for small game? Enough to penetrate whatever skin, feathers, or bone protects your *toughest* quarry's heart, lungs, or brain, and to terminate the functioning of those organs upon arrival.

How does that translate to fpe? How much fpe must the weapon generate for small game? It should be understood that the British routinely take rabbits, squirrels, rats, pigeons, and other birds and mammals of similar size using airguns generating the legal limit of 12 fpe at the muzzle. They take these critters *with well-placed shots* at ranges to 40 yards, and those pellets have shed a lot of energy by the time they've reached the quarry. So, let's use 12 fpe as the minimum muzzle energy required of an air rifle or pistol used for small game hunting.

How does one recognize such an airgun? By knowing the weight and velocity of the pellet leaving its muzzle. For example, any airgun that can launch a .177 pellet of 9 grains at 775 fps, or a .22 pellet of 14 grains at 625 fps, can kill the animals listed above out to 30 yards (a conservative estimate) if the pellet hits a vital area. Those velocities can be reduced somewhat by using heavier pellets in order to reach that 12-fpe minimum requirement. For example, a 10.5-grain .177 pellet traveling at 720 fps will also reach the 12 fpe minimum. For squirrels, however, it's advisable to get a gun with more than 12 fpe, or keep the ranges to less than 20 yards and be sure to hit a vital area (brain or heart/lung). As any veteran squirrel hunter will tell you, "they take a lot of killing."

Caliber. Which caliber is best for small game? There are good arguments for .177, .20, .22, .and .25, but the fact remains: it is the *energy* carried by the pellet and transmitted to the vital organs that does the killing. If your primary target is the ubiquitous pigeon or starling, a high-speed .177 is all you'll need, so there's little point in the extra expense of the larger calibers. It was once argued that the heavier calibers had a more curved trajectory than a flat-shooting .177 - requiring more hold-over when aiming at distant targets - but that doesn't apply to the high-velocity .22s being manufactured today, many of which will shoot nearly flat out to 40 or 50 yards. Another slogan was ".177 for feathers, .22 for fur." Don't tell that to the millions of rabbits that have fallen to .177 pellets, many of which approach the weight of the lighter .22 pellets. The .20 has always been considered a credible compromise between .177 and .22, offering both a flat trajectory and smackdown energy approaching the .22. The .20 Sheridan rifle, for example, remains one of the best small-game killers ever devised. If rabbits are the primary target, however, be advised that a .177 zipping along at nearly 1000 fps can completely "icepick" through the rodent's chest, allowing it to hop away with a quizzical expression, whereas a heavier caliber would have created a larger wound cavity and knocked the animal flat. The .25- and .30-caliber airguns, especially PCP rifles and heavy-duty springers, are effective killers in the right hands, but are probably a poor choice for the average small-game hunter.

Today, many air weapons easily attain that minimum 12 fpe, and hunters living in free countries or states can purchase, without licenses or bureaucratic harassment, airguns that far exceed 12 fpe (particularly the PCPs). Look at the packaging for spring rifles at your local shop and you'll see velocities printed in 3-inch letters touting 1200 fps or more. Such airguns could extend the small-game hunting ranges to 60 or 70 yards (and over 100 yards with the PCPs).

CO_2 Power in Hunting Use. CO_2 rifles and some custom gas pistols can generate the minimum 12 fpe, but be advised that small game hunting takes place most often in the cooler months. Unless fitted with special valves, CO_2 guns lose too much power in sub-60°F weather (i.e., during Fall and Winter in the Northern Hemisphere) to be effective hunting tools. Conversely, CO_2 gas pressure increases in warmer temperatures, which leads to increased velocity.

Single-Stroke Pneumatics. Excluding some obsolete airweapons like the Genesis, there are currently no single-stroke pneumatics that are truly viable small-game hunting weapons.

There is a tendency among hunters new to airgunning to reach for the most powerful weapon available, but before they pay money for that springer generating 30 fpe, they should know that a magnum blaster may be an unwise choice. . .

Ergonomics. High-powered spring guns tend to be long, heavy, and hard to cock, whereas their lower-powered siblings are light and handy and can still deliver game-killing power. The big springers also have a jarring, uncomfortable firing sequence that will soon make the shooter long for that smoother, lower-powered weapon he passed up. The size, weight, and behavior of an airgun are important factors in the purchasing decision, especially if one's hunting involves long treks afield. If size, weight, cocking force, and shooting behavior are important to you, consider a lower-powered spring gun, a PCP, or a pump pneumatic. The PCP will require the hunter to carry charging paraphernalia (a hand pump or spare tank) into the field, but the reservoir may hold enough air for the number of shots one expects to take; a squirrel hunter, for example, may take no

more than a dozen shots in a day's jaunt. Some of the better PCPs can be "dialed down" to reduce velocity, noise, and carry range, and this has the added value of increasing the number of shots per fill from the onboard reservoir. In fact, if there is such a thing as a multi-purpose airgun, such a PCP might qualify. It can be used for relatively quiet backyard shooting, small game hunting, metallic silhouette, field target shooting, and – when dialed up – for hunting game the size of raccoons, coyotes, and feral hogs.

Excess Power. Those magnum spring guns tend to be expensive scope destroyers with springs that often need replacement after a few thousand shots. And what happens to that blistering 1300-fps pellet (no matter what type of powerplant launched it) after it's drilled its way through that pigeon's head and is still zipping along at 800 fps? Will it bury itself in roof rafters or shingles - or your neighbor's aluminum siding? Will it break a window two hundred yards away? Such questions must be asked when purchasing an airgun to be used in a populated area. Some hunters avoid the spring gun for hunting because they believe that leaving the spring cocked for extended periods of time will cause it to take a "set." This may have validity with guns in the magnum range, but is less likely to occur with unstressed, medium-power spring guns.

Noise. Noise is an important consideration. PCPs and pump pneumatics are louder than spring guns, sometimes as loud as a .22 firearm. A quiet field gun is less alarming to game than a noisy one and could result in a heavier game bag, but a quiet gun has obvious benefit to the backyard hunter as well. Silencers are an option available to airgunning hunters living in countries where they're legal. They are of little advantage on a spring gun that generates a lot of mechanical noise, but they can reduce the report of a PCP, pump, or CO_2 gun to a mere *pfft*. The squirrel hunter who sits still and occasionally emits a sound no louder than mouse flatulence can usually take more squirrels from a productive spot than a noisy hunter with an itch to immediately retrieve every animal he drops. The silencer may be a factory-fitted, integral, non-removable component of the gun, an aftermarket purchase, or a home-made device.

Hunting Large Game

"Big-bore" PCPs in calibers ranging from .30 to .60 are commercially produced in countries where the hunting population is forbidden to own firearms (principally, Korea and the Philippines). There are also a number of custom airgun fabricators who make PCP rifles that can generate upwards of 500 fpe. Such guns can take feral hogs, coyotes, raccoons, and small deer and antelope. Additionally, they are legally sanctioned for deer hunting in several of the United States. Such guns use air pressurized to 3000 – 4500 psi and ball or conical projectiles of approximately 150 grains. If the airgunner is after game of a size similar to the animals mentioned, only a PCP can handle the chore. In fact, many airgunners decry using airguns for this type of hunting, citing the fact that even the famed 30-30 deer rifle – considered to be at the low end of deer-hunting power – launches a 170-grain bullet at 2300 fps to generate 2000 fpe.

Plinking

The ideal plinking airgun will be a repeater that shoots cheaply. Recall from the chapter on plinking that this type of shooting could easily expend a hundred shots or more per session. No one wants to cock a breakbarrel spring gun for that many shots, much less pump up a pneumatic. A Daisy BB gun may be a suitable, easy-cocking spring gun if the targets are tin cans, but not bottles, which will invariably send the BBs back to the shooter. For that duty, select a repeating CO_2 rifle or pistol that shoots soft lead pellets. To add to the fun factor, get one of the repeating pistols equipped with a laser sight. There are BB machine pistols available that can really multiply the fun factor. For those with a good degree of disposable income, the Shooting Star Company will sell, for home use, the same shooting gallery setup they provide to carnivals. This includes the Thompson-style machine gun, the ammo, the electric compressor, the targets and backstop, and repair parts. Some of these ultra-durable

guns have been in continuous operation for 30 years or more.

Training

For decades, airguns have been used by parents, schools, and police and military organizations to teach correct gun handling. Airguns are not harmless, of course, but an errant pellet from a CO_2 revolver will have far less consequence than a bullet coming from a .22 firearm, the gun that is often selected as a training weapon. If your objective is to introduce a youth to the fun and responsibilities associated with shooting, select a rifle or pistol that requires no pumping or onerous, repetitive cocking. This simplifies the shooting session and enables student and teacher to concentrate on safe gun-handling procedures and the intricate holding, breathing, sighting, and squeezing activities that send a projectile into the target. If the trainees are young, the rifle or pistol should be sized appropriately, so it's advisable to bring the individual along for the purchase and allow him or her to shoulder the rifle or raise the pistol. There's nothing more discouraging to a youngster to have to tuck the stock under his or her armpit, rather than correctly press it into the cup of the shoulder, in order to reach the trigger and align the sights.

Target Shooting

Selection of an airgun for target shooting depends on:

- The type of target shooting one intends to pursue (10-meter rifle, 10-meter pistol, silhouette, field target, benchrest, etc);
- The level of venue in which the shooter will participate (solitary basement or backyard shooting; matches at the local range; formal international competitions, etc.);
- The level of dedication brought to the hobby;
- The budget allotted for the airgun.

No matter what type of target shooting one intends to pursue, a general rule applies: *The gun has to be more accurate than the shooter.* A beginner should know that most any target airgun will be capable of delivering a greater level of accuracy than he or she can tap. At this stage, it's wiser for that beginner to get an inexpensive rifle or pistol and "see how things go" rather than immediately purchase an Olympic contender for a few thousand dollars. Here's why . . .

The beginner may purchase a $250 single-stroke pneumatic target rifle and set about learning the rudiments of breathing, sight picture, and trigger release. He will experience excitement and a real sense of accomplishment watching his scores gradually rise as his technique improves. There will come a time, however, if he or she is properly coached and sufficiently dedicated, when the scores seem to "plateau." He may not be able to score any better than, say, 96/100. The problem may lie with the gun, not the shooter. The gun simply may not be capable of consistently hitting the ten ring shot after shot. When firing a 10-shot group from a rest, which eliminates shooter-induced error, the air rifle may only be capable of scoring a maximum of 96. In this case, the shooter's capability has probably exceeded what the gun can deliver. Now what?

The shooter has to decide how far he or she wants to go with this hobby. A more accurate gun – whether it's a ten meter air rifle or a whizz-bang field target contraption – may cost a couple of thousand dollars. Only the shooter can decide if the expenditure is worth it. If our paper-puncher with the $250 SSP wants to get to the next level, but can't afford a gun that can win Olympic gold, there are used guns that were *former* Olympic winners that are no longer competitive but are still "better" than the shooter's current capability. Such guns, particularly the Feinwerkbau recoilless spring guns and other types made by Anschutz, Walther, Hammerli, and Weihrauch, can be had for several hundred dollars and are accurate enough to carry the targeteer to the next level. The shooter may also find that these older target guns – with their figured walnut stocks and deeply blued metalwork – have an intrinsic appeal that their more modern, but sterile, counter-parts cannot provide.

Those shooters entering the field target, bench-rest, 10-meter, and silhouette shooting games would be well advised to find a club in their locale specializing in those types of shooting. This is where the competitions will take place; additionally, there is no better way to determine what type of equipment is needed for each class or level, or how big an investment will be required to participate effectively, not only in terms of money, but in dedication and discipline. Spectating at a match or two will give a good indication of what guns and ancillary equipment are winning the contests. Although there are exceptions to the rule, most participants in the airgun shooting sports are willing to share information with interested newcomers, and the more informal matches often have opportunities before and after matches for gabfests (sometimes accompanied by beer and barbecue).

COST

It's no secret that high quality airguns have always cost more than mass-produced airguns. For decades, the English, Germans, and Swiss produced airguns that were of demonstrably higher quality than American airguns and their cost was commensurate with their quality. One has only to compare an English Webley Mark III underlever from the 1960s to an American Crosman or Benjamin of the same period, and it will be readily apparent why one could buy four Crosmans or Benjamins for the price of one Webley. The Webley is made of walnut and hand-fitted, machined steel - highly polished and deeply blued. The Crosman is made of beech, steel where it counts, and various bits of plastic. This does not mean the Crosman was an inferior airgun. In terms of accuracy and power, the Crosman pumpers of the 1960s equaled the accuracy of the Webley and exceeded its power. This was also true of the Benjamins and Sheridans of the time. In fact, Sheridan once produced a pump gun that was probably of higher build quality than the Webley, and beat the Webley in power and accuracy as well. That was the Sheridan Supergrade, but it didn't last long in the market. Americans had little incentive to buy a gun that cost more than, say, the exceptional Winchester Model 52 .22 rimfire of that period – and had nowhere near the power or range of the firearm. Europeans, on the other hand, were, and are, suffering under repressive government regulations that severely limit firearms ownership, so they bought the next best thing – an airgun. Many of those European manufacturers built firearms of very high quality (mainly for export) and they lavished the same attention on the airguns they sold to their beleaguered countrymen.

American interest in airgunning has grown with the increase in firearms laws and the decrease in available shooting lands. In the 1960s, a visionary in West Virginia saw that Americans would probably appreciate something better in airguns than the mass-produced fodder they'd been sold for decades. This was Robert Law, who founded Air Rifle Headquarters. His mail order company and informative monthly newsletter singlehandedly introduced Americans to the finest airguns produced in Europe. Suddenly, Americans began to see that an airgun was not a weak substitute for a firearm or a toy to mollify little boys until they were old enough to get a "real" gun. They were intricate, sophisticated, beautiful weapons designed for short-range shooting. Not only were they *not* inferior to firearms, they were in many cases superior to them in terms of materials, workmanship, fitting, and accuracy.

It would be easy to say that, when buying an airgun, *you get what you pay for* and leave it at that – but that's not quite true. Something new has entered the airgunning scene: chinese clones of European airguns that sell for a fraction of the cost of the originals.

These chinese knockoffs are nut and bolt copies of some of Europe's and America's finest airguns. Although they are inferior to the originals in fit and finish, they are equal to the originals in performance. Built in communist factories unhampered by labor or environmental laws, advantaged by low-paid workers, a weak dollar, and immunity to patent infringement lawsuits, these cheap offerings have become very popular and there are many online dealers selling them. Many of the buyers are willing and able to refinish the guns internally and externally to

a very high standard, and a cottage industry of custom stock makers has evolved that will replace the varnished board of the clone with a beautiful duplicate in walnut or fiddleback maple. Additionally, there are websites and online forums devoted exclusively to the many varieties of these airweapons.

So, although cost is still fairly commensurate with quality, it is quite possible to spend little and get an airgun that shoots as well, or better, than a higher-priced model. The cheaper gun may have a "polymer" stock rather than finely grained walnut, and there may be more plastic and castings rather than machined steel, but the perforated rabbits and tin cans won't know the difference.

MAINTENANCE

Airguns of any type are easy to maintain, especially when compared to firearms. They don't use corrosive gunpowders or priming material, so the barrels won't usually need to be cleaned of leading or fouling, as typically happens with firearms. Be advised, however, that leading can be an issue with high-powered PCPs, and it is for this reason that PCP shooters lubricate their pellets. Airguns with steel barrels will, obviously, require an occasional pass with an oiled patch to keep them from rusting. This treatment is unnecessary with the brass barrels used in some CO_2 and pump guns. Pass a magnet over the barrel; if the magnet "sticks," the barrel is ferrous and *will* rust – inside and out - if it isn't oiled. Be advised that some guns have an outer shroud of either plastic or alloy, with an inner barrel that is steel. These will require oiling.

Spring guns will require piston lubrication to keep them operating at peak performance. Break-barrel springers will need exterior protection where sweaty hands grasp the barrel for cocking (this can be as simple as applying a hard coat of clear car wax, or wiping it occasionally with an oily rag). The springs may also require a thin coating of grease (sometimes sold as "spring tar") to reduce noise and promote a smooth firing sequence. Applying the grease may require dismantling the gun, something many owners won't be willing to tackle.

Single-stroke pneumatics will require care similar to that required for pump pneumatics, an occasional drop of oil here or there to keep the seals operable, but the PCPs have ancillary equipment (tanks, valves, fittings, and/or pumps) that will also require regular maintenance. There are also safety rules that must be strictly observed when handling the PCP's high-pressure components.

Air cartridge guns, *per se*, are relatively easy to maintain. They don't compress or store gas - they release it. The cartridges themselves, which are miniature high-pressure tanks, will require seal lubrication and an occasional rebuild. Additionally, as this is currently an obsolete power system, finding parts will gradually become more difficult as time passes.

THE HASSLE FACTOR

Many airgunners recall their first Daisy as a simple device requiring no more attention than a fill-up with BBs from a cardboard tube and an occasional drop of 3-in-One® oil in a well-marked hole ("Oil Here"). They came to expect the same low-maintenance, ease-of-use of their later airguns, perhaps bemoaning the fact that their new pump gun, although a real powerhouse, now required sweat, as well as costlier ammo. And many airgunners simply shunned those newfangled CO_2 guns that actually needed to be filled from a separate tank, a tank that had be taken to special re-fill stations when empty. The later CO_2 gas cartridge guns were equally suspect. The gas cartridges provided easy power, but were an added expense, had the potential to leak, and required that the seals in the bowels of the gun be kept in proper condition. Clearly, something more complex was going on inside these new-style guns, and, if they did break down, there was that ominous warning in the manual: "Do not attempt to dismantle this gun; send to an authorized repair station." Repair station? Authorized? Yes, there was a list of them enclosed with the gun. "And be sure to package securely..."

The point is, before making an airgun purchase, one should know exactly what the prospective gun requires in terms of ammunition, power supply, maintenance,

and repair. Some airguns may offer very high levels of accuracy and power, but may be too much of a hassle for the average airgunner.

Ammunition. That potent .25 or .30 caliber PCP is a real masterblaster, but are pellets readily available for it? What about a *variety* of pellets? Some guns shoot best with only one style or brand of pellet, and the way to determine that is to try as many as are available. There are dozens of pellets available in .177 and .22 (and, to a lesser degree, .20), but the selection starts to thin when it comes to the more exotic airgun calibers. Before purchasing an airgun in an unusual caliber, do some research on the availability of pellets. Some airguns shoot pellets produced by a single manufacturer located on the other side of the globe. Some airguns are so specialized that they come with moulds that the owner must use to cast ammo specific to that gun.

The same ammo consideration applies to vintage airguns. Although it is true that some of the old .177 and .22 airguns are shooting better now because of the availability of better pellets, there are some guns that shoot projectiles that may be difficult to find. How about those .21 caliber Crosmans? They're wonderful old bulk-fillers, but just where do you get pellets for them? And that Apache pump rifle from the 1950s is an accurate and powerful airgun, but it shoots .25 caliber balls. Would you know where to get them? You would, if you ever owned a vintage Korean Yewha foot-pump air shotgun with a .25-caliber bore. That beast fired both shotshells and single .25 balls, which you purchased cheaply, in bulk, by buying #4 swaged buckshot. They work just as well in the Apache. The point is, most airgun ammo can be found, but it may not be available at the local discount outlet. Be prepared for that reality if you plan on purchasing an airgun in any caliber other than .177, .20, or .22.

Power Source. Some sources of power for airguns present a greater hassle factor than others. The buyer should be fully aware of what will be needed to "power-up" the prospective purchase, and decide beforehand whether he or she is willing to deal with it.

When modern PCPs hit the airgunning scene, they were not universally embraced. Many airgunners accustomed to traditional sources of airgun power were put off by these new (and expensive) creations. They weren't skeptical of the power source, per se – after all, there's nothing revolutionary about an airgun powered by pressurized air. They were bothered by the complexities of charging the guns. They required the shooter to purchase a SCUBA tank, of all things, as well as high-pressure hoses, valves, and something called a *yoke*. Plus, the tanks had to be refilled at skindiving shops, and, unless the shooter was a certified diver, the shop wouldn't refill it. Some shooter's actually took lessons and became certified skindivers simply to get access to the shop's air compressor (the diving lessons were cheaper than a compressor, apparently). In time, the refill issue was eased somewhat by dive-shops willing to fill tanks for airgunners who signed legal affidavits promising not to use the tanks for breathing purposes. Some shooters purchased their own gas- or electric-powered compressors, and then airgun shops saw the profit potential in the refill business and invested in their own compressors. Some shooters were (and are) willing to invest time, energy, and money *on an ongoing basis* because of the high performance of their PCP guns, but many more airgunners have decided to stick to guns with less demanding power systems. Each group weighs the advantages and disadvantages and makes an informed choice.

Each type of airgun power system has characteristics that should be considered prior to purchase:

Springs: Springs can weaken, but unless the gun is in the magnum class (~900 fps in .177 and 800 in .22), the gun should be good for many thousands of shots before power begins to decline. Some of the really potent spring guns, however, have been known to need spring replacement after a couple of thousand shots. However, replacing the spring is not too complex an undertaking for someone with a spring compressor and average mechanical ability, and there are replacements available from airgunsmiths that are superior in strength and longevity to the originals.

Some of the "mild" spring guns from the past barely stressed their powerplants, and many of them retain serviceable original springs even after many decades of use. These lower-powered guns are also quite pleasant to shoot, having none of the jarring recoil of the magnums.

Another factor to consider when purchasing a springer is the force required to cock the gun. Some of the magnum guns can require over 50 pounds of effort. This is a function of the power of the spring as well as the length of the barrel. Some spring guns can be really tiresome to cock repeatedly over a lengthy shooting session. Try out the gun, if possible, before purchasing it, then ask yourself if you could cock it over and over during a typical shooting session. Even if it's a real bear to cock, requiring two hands with the buttstock jammed in the crotch, it still may be a viable purchase if it's going to be used for, say, hunting rather than plinking, where the number of shots won't be too taxing. In this regard, the "carbine" versions of an air rifle, when offered, will prove more difficult to cock because the cocking lever (i.e., the barrel) is shorter. The same principle applies to spring pistols.

Gas "Spring": This is not actually a spring, of course, but a cylinder in which air or some other gas is compressed and held prior to the shot. Some have adjustable power, which increases or decreases cocking effort as well as velocity, but this feature involves purchasing a separate hand pump. In other applications (automotive trunk and hood lifts, for example) these devices have proven reliability. Although they're reliable in airguns, they have been known to fail (i.e., leak). When this happens, they usually require the services of an expert for dismantling and repair.

CO_2: A bulk-fill CO_2 gun (one that does not use small disposable cartridges) will require a separate CO_2 tank to fill its onboard reservoir. These tanks come in a variety of sizes ranging from 3.5 oz. to 20 lbs. The larger tanks are often used to fill the smaller tanks, which are not too cumbersome to carry afield and can provide hundreds of shots. Purchasing and filling these tanks contributes to the hassle factor of these guns, but once the equipment is purchased and the charging procedure is learned, it is an extremely economical power source, far cheaper than using CO_2 from disposable cartridges. Additionally, the guns that use bulk fill CO_2, particularly the vintage Crosmans, are more powerful, accurate, and better made, than their modern counterparts.

The charging procedure, as described in the section on CO_2 guns, is not too difficult to learn, but it is not as easy as popping in a "powerlet." Some of the new and old CO_2 guns can be used with both cartridge and bulk-fill CO_2 by using special cylinder caps sold by airgun shops. Refilling the large CO_2 tank can be done at paintballer shops, welding supply houses, fire extinguisher suppliers, and beverage retailers supplying CO_2 for restaurants and soda fountains.

Guns using disposable CO_2 cartridges present an added cost, but they save the user the strain of pumping up the gun, or cocking a heavy spring, and they've become very reliable since their introduction in the early 1950s.

Some vintage CO_2 guns such as the Schimel and early Benjamins, use 8-gram CO_2 cartridges. Don't pass up one of these gems simply because you don't know where to get gas for it. These smaller cartridges are not as readily available as the 12-gram cartridges produced today, but they can often be found in kitchen supply shops (to power seltzer bottles), and in luggage shops that sell traveling "bars" that use seltzer bottles. And an online search will produce many mail-order suppliers for these smaller capsules.

AIRGUN REPAIR FACILITIES

No prospective airgunner should be put off by the possibility of not finding a suitable repair facility for whatever airgun he or she buys. Not only are manufacturers willing to warrant their products and take them in for repair when necessary, but there are many private shops that will repair, restore, or customize airguns of any type - vintage or modern. In fact, skilled customizers have become so prevalent, that one major American manufacturer has decided to open up a custom shop of its own. Customers can take a standard model and specify various caliber, stock, sights, or barrel lengths, making the gun a truly individualized piece. Virtually all airgun shops have websites indicating their specialties. One has only to get onto any of the established airgun forums to find links to their sites. Additionally, these forums tend to be excellent places to get reviews of the relative performance of the airgun repair facilities.

Index

R

rabbit, 41, 57, 81, *82*, 101, 106, 110, 124, 131, 132, 153, 154
raccoon, 47, 51
rangefinding, 85, 161, 164
rear sight, 69, 70, 73, 82, 95, 109
receiver, 14, 19, 39, 44, 51, 58, 69, 81, *82*, 84, 86, 92, 102, 108, 109
recoil, 15, 84
recoil-cancelling, 16
recoilless, 18, 19, 21, 22, 41, 51, 55, 56, 70, 84, 106, 192
red dot, 70, 74, 75, 91, 92, 96, 97, 101, 117
Red Ryder, 13
regulator, 48
repeater, 13, 27, 33, 34, 41, 116, 153, 191
reservoir, 13, 27, 28, 31, 32, 40, 41, 47, 48, 51, 52, 55, 56, 190, 195
reticle, 80, 81, *83*, 84, 91, 101, 144, 145, 165
rheostat, 91, 102
ricochets, 118
rifling, 5, 6, 8, 14, 20, 23, 36, 44, 65
rimfires, 1, 79
rings, 83
Robert Law, 193
Roundheads, 6
Running Target, 175, 177
rust, 21, 22, 23, 24, 33, 35, 36, 44, 52, 58, 193

S

sampler pack, 108
sampler pack., 6
Saxby Palmer, 61, 62
Schimel, 29, 196
scope, 16, 51, 62, 70, 74, 79, 80, 81, 82, 83, 84, 85, 86, 87, 91, 92, 101, 105, 106, 108, 109, 110, 116, *132*, 144, 145, 150, 162, 164, 165, 190
scope base, 86
Scope caps, 83
scope creep, 16
scope stop, 16
screw caps, 35
SCUBA, 39, 47, 48, 49, 50, 52, 61, 195
seal failure, 35, 57
sear, 13, 14, 15, 16, 20, 22, 28, 33, 39, 41, 43, 48, 49, 51, 55, 56, 62, 97, 163
semi-automatic, 34, 50, 117
semi-automatics, 34, 116
sentinel, 153
Sheridan, 1, 7, 42, 47, 69, 82, 183, 185, 187, 189, 192
Sheridan Supergrade, 192
shim, 84
Shooting Star Company, 191
shot placement, 124
shotgun scopes, 84
shotguns, 8, 39, 185
shoulder stocks, 86
sidecocking, 19
sidelever, 14

sight, 17, 55, 56, 65, 69, 70, 73, 74, 75, 79, 80, 82, 91, 92, 95, 96, 101, 102, 105, 106, 107, 108, 109, 110, 117, 119, 126, 144, 149, 150, 153, 161, 162, 164, 191, 192
sight picture, 69, 74
sight radius, 73
sighting-in, 69, 70, 96, 105, 106, 108, 109
silencer, 150, 191
Silver Streaks, 183
single-action, 34
single-shot, 13, 29, 33, 34, 41, 96, 116, 131, 183
single-stroke, 48, 190, 192
siphon, 31
skirt, 5, 14
sledge system, 19, 84
small game, 13, 41, 55, 56, 85, 86, 124, 126, 131, 183, 189, 190
Smith and Wesson, 35
solvent, 52, 85
sparrow, 149
sporter, 13, 16, 21, 22, 75, 153, 162
spotting scope, 108
Spring, 13, 14, 15, 16, 17, 18, 22, 50, 84, 108, 193, 195
spring guides, 18, 22
spring-dampening, 22
squads, 161
squirrel, 80, 91, 108, 110, 124, 131, 135, 136, 137, 189, 190
stalking, 132
still hunting, 57
stock, 16, 17, 19, 22, 23, 52, 56, 58, 73, 84, 92, 105, 108, 116, 162, 176, 191, 193, 196
stop-blocks, 84
suet, 150
sweet spot, 107
synthetic seals, 21

T

tang, 73
tap, 13, 21, 97, 110, 137, 192
target acquisition, 70, 92, 101, 144, 165
temperature, 16, 27, 30, 41, 55, 56
theft detection powder, 145
training, 5, 34, 191
trajectory, 84, 85, 110, 126, 149, 162, 189
transfer port, 14, 16, 57
trigger, 13, 14, 15, 16, 17, **20**, 21, 22, 23, 28, 29, 33, 34, 39, 40, 41, 43, 44, 48, 51, 52, 55, 56, 58, 62, 65, 80, 91, 95, 96, 97, 107, 116, 119, 136, 144, 191, 192
trigger guard, 29, 95, 107
trigger pull, 34, 40
Tube diameter, 91
Tuning, 17
turrets, 80, 83
TV cameras, 108
two-way recoil, 84

U

ultraviolet light, 145

V

valve stem, 28, 33, 39, 41, 42, 48, 51, 56, 61, 62
variable, 41, 81, *83*, 87, 110, 165
variable power scope, 83
velocity, 5, 7, 8, 15, 17, 20, 22, 23, 27, 42, 44, 47, 49,
    50, 51, 52, 55, 56, 57, 107, 108, 125, 126, 144,
    149, 187, 189, 190, 195
vent hole, 21
vermin, 18, 143, 153, 154
Vincent, 8, 39

W

wadcutter, 6, 95
Walther, 1, 55, 61, 192

wasp-waisted, 5
wax, 24, 36, 44, 58, 193
Weaver, 92, 96, 102
Webley Mark III, 183, 192
whistle, 137, 149
windage, 69, 73, 74, 75, 80, 83, 84, 85, 86, 87, 91, 95,
    96, 105, 106, 108, 109, 110, 165
woodchuck, 51
wound channel, 7, 144
wrist, 17, 107, 116

Y

Yewha, 8, 194
yoke, 32, 195

Z

zero, 49, 70, 74, 105
zeroing, 69, 105, 106, 107, 108

Lightning Source UK Ltd.
Milton Keynes UK
UKOW042106220911

179138UK00004B/6/P